Critical Guides to French Texts

44 Vigny: Les Destinées

Critical Guides to French Texts

EDITED BY ROGER LITTLE, WOLFGANG VAN EMDEN, DAVID WILLIAMS

Students and External Readers	Staff & Research Students
DATE DUE FOR RETURN	**DATE OF ISSUE**
12.MAR 96 8900	30. 06. 88
25. 06. 86.	14. 12. 88
08. 12. 86. 20. 03. 89	29. 06. 89
24. 06. 87	19. 03. 90
21. 03. 88.	28. 06 '90
30. 06. 88	N.B. All books must be returned for the Annual Inspection in June

Any book which you borrow remains your responsibility until the loan slip is cancelled

VIGNY

Les Destinées

Keith Wren

Lecturer in European Studies
University of Kent, Canterbury

Grant & Cutler Ltd
1985

ISBN 0 7293 0188 5

I.S.B.N. 84-599-0401-6

DEPÓSITO LEGAL: V. 298 - 1985

Printed in Spain by
Artes Gráficas Soler, S.A., Valencia
for
GRANT & CUTLER LTD
11 BUCKINGHAM STREET, LONDON W.C.2

Contents

Acknowledgments

I owe a debt of gratitude to Professor Roger Little, the co-editor of the series, for his assistance in the gestation of this monograph; to my colleague Dr Susan Taylor-Horrex, who read the manuscript, made many useful suggestions, and suitably encouraging noises at critical junctures; and to Mrs Janet Howarth, who uncomplainingly deciphered my delphic typescript, and typed the final version with efficiency, accuracy and speed.

Note on Editions Used

Although several good individual editions of *Les Destinées* are currently available, I have chosen to use for my reference edition the volume in the Gallimard 'Poésie' series established by André Jarry and introduced by Marcel Arland which comprises both *Les Destinées* and the earlier *Poèmes antiques et modernes*. The text used in this edition is an advance on that printed in most of the others, since it incorporates the results of recent research on the manuscripts of the poems. The annotation in this edition is also more helpful than that contained in the later edition by J.-P. Saint-Gérand (Paris, Garnier-Flammarion, 1978), although this contains a much wider selection of *disjecta membra* together with some fascinating and unusual 'Archives de l'œuvre'. Of the individual editions of *Les Destinées*, my personal preference is for that of P.-G. Castex (Paris, SEDES, 1968), but those by V.-L. Saulnier (Geneva, Droz, 1946), Alphonse Bouvet (Paris, Bordas, 1971) and Maurice Tournier (Paris, Larousse, 1972) are all fully and carefully annotated and have much to recommend them.

For my references to Vigny's other works, I have used the edition of *Œuvres complètes* by Fernand Baldensperger (Paris, Pléiade, 1948-50, 2 vols). This is quite frankly rather super-annuated, and a replacement edition by François Germain and André Jarry is awaited. The one-volume edition by Paul Viallaneix in the 'Intégrale' series (Paris, Seuil, 1965) would be greatly preferable to the Pléiade if only it included the *Journal*. Finally, the works collected as the *Mémoires inédits* by Jean Sangnier (Paris, Gallimard, 1958) constitute an indispensable supplement to the *Journal*, particularly because of the numerous 'Fragments et projets' that the volume contains.

Note on Abbreviations and Proper Names

In order to ensure complete clarity, all references to specific lines in the poems of *Les Destinées* are preceded by a letter (or letters) indicating the title of the poem. These abbreviations are as follows:

AOA.	L'Age d'or de l'avenir
BM.	La Bouteille à la mer
CS.	La Colère de Samson
D.	Les Destinées
EP.	L'Esprit pur
F.	La Flûte
MB.	La Maison du berger
ML.	La Mort du loup
MO.	Le Mont des oliviers
O.	Les Oracles
S.	La Sauvage
W.	Wanda

At the risk of inconsistency, I have tended to anglicise the proper names of major historical and religious figures (such as Jehovah and Jesus), where retention of the French form seemed needlessly artificial. In the few remaining cases, I have opted for the French form, e.g. Dalila rather than Delilah, Destinées rather than Fates (or whatever) etc.

Introduction

Vigny's reputation as a poet in the eyes of posterity rests primarily on *Les Destinées*, published posthumously in 1864 by his literary executor Louis de Ratisbonne. It is a collection of poems which the author himself had prepared for publication, and despite certain dissenting views, it may be argued that it stands complete in itself in terms of internal logic and overall coherence. Nonetheless, since one of the hallmarks of literary Romanticism is individual self-expression, it is true to say that some awareness of an author's life and background can enrich our understanding of his work, and in this context some brief remarks on Vigny's own history and his previous poetic output insofar as they impinge on *Les Destinées* may be useful. The pessimism that pervades his work, to the extent that it may be termed a characteristic of it, derives as much from personal circumstance as from poetic temperament, and the optimism which constitutes his final world-view, far from being a late flowering of the 1840s and 1850s, is already in germ in some of his earliest poetry.

Vigny's life seems to have been a constant catalogue of misfortunes, a series of embittering failures and disappointments that required all his considerable moral resilience to transcend. He was born in 1797 into an aristocratic family impoverished by the Revolution, and his early life as the only surviving child of a weak and ageing father and a domineering mother may be seen to have fuelled that resentment against the cosmic order which marks so much of his poetry. A hypersensitive boy, he was persecuted at school for being too clever, too pretty and a member of the hereditary nobility in a post-revolutionary age. This consciousness of belonging to a 'race maudite' (*7*, II, p.1260) was compounded by his subsequent failure in the choice of a career. Despite his enthusiasm for military life, the traditional means by which the nobility had made their mark in the pre-revolutionary world, he had mistaken his vocation: 'J'avais porté dans une vie tout active une nature toute contemplative' (7, II, p.527). This sense of inadequacy dogged him for long after he had finally left the army in 1827, to the extent that, despite his view that 'l'homme d'action n'est qu'un penseur manqué' (7, II, p.890), he never ceased secretly to wish to play a major active role in public life, and felt slighted by the refusal of successive monarchs fully to recognise his gifts. He also mistook his way in his emotional life, marrying the unhappy Englishwoman Lydia Bunbury, who brought him neither the companionship he craved, nor the money he needed, nor the children he hoped would perpetuate the family name.

In this period of his life the two main features of his literary career are the Scott-influenced historical novel *Cinq-Mars* (1826), and the poems collectively known as *Poèmes antiques et modernes* published at various junctures between 1822 and 1831. The salient aspect of both is the glorification of resistance to tyranny, a tyranny embodied by Richelieu in the novel and by God in the most significant poems. And while *Cinq-Mars* is indubitably rather a dull novel, some of the poems are memorably far from dullness. Anatole France thought 'Moïse' the finest poem in French, a palm Théophile Gautier preferred to bestow on 'Eloa', and there are fine passages in 'Le Déluge', 'La Prison' and 'Le Trappiste'. All these poems vibrate with intensely personal involvement. Two interrelated themes predominate — that of the heroic and defiant outcast, and that of the beauty of self-sacrifice to an ideal. The first is epitomised in the resistance to a God perceived as malevolent (because inscrutable) manifested by the prisoner in 'La Prison', by Emmanuel in 'Le Déluge', by Satan in 'Eloa', and perhaps most enduringly by the eponymous hero of 'Moïse', of whom Vigny wrote (in a letter of 24 December 1838 to Camilla Maunoir):

Ce grand nom ne sert que de masque à un homme de tous les siècles et plus moderne qu'antique: l'homme de génie, las de son eternel veuvage et désespéré de voir sa solitude plus vaste à mesure qu'il grandit. Fatigué de sa grandeur, il demande le néant. (*I*, p.274)

This rejection of the prevailing world-order, extending to the indictment of God himself, prefigures several poems of *Les Destinées*, such as 'La Mort du loup', 'Les Oracles', 'Wanda', and the greatest of the poems of revolt, 'Le Mont des oliviers'. The related theme of sacrifice, although less forcefully stated, is nonetheless clearly apparent. Emmanuel sacrifices himself to save his beloved Sara in 'Le Déluge', the Trappist monk sacrifices himself and his followers to save his King in 'Le Trappiste', and Eloa, the angel of pity (a supremely human characteristic for Vigny), sacrifices herself to save Satan, to the accompaniment of two of Vigny's most poignant lines:

Gloire dans l'Univers, dans les Temps, à celui
Qui s'immole à jamais pour le salut d'autrui.

('Eloa', 757-58)

Vigny's point is that sacrifice does not necessarily produce positive results — all the examples quoted above are fruitless — but is intrinsically admirable in itself. *Cinq-Mars* similarly illustrates the precept of 'la beauté du sacrifice de soi-même à une généreuse pensée' (7, II, p.19), and an observation in the *Journal* stresses that 'le sacrifice est ce qu'il y a de plus beau au monde' (7, II, p.890). Trapped as he was in an unfulfilling career and an inadequate marriage, it is easy to understand at one and the same time Vigny's consuming pessimism and his desperate need to believe in an ideal. Not until 1854, in 'La Bouteille à la mer' is he genuinely able to achieve the ideal of self-sacrifice with a positive purpose in his creative writing.

As the 1820s gave way to the 1830s, Vigny found himself further and further adrift. His old political loyalties to the crown were extinct, yet he spurned the bourgeois monarchy of Louis-Philippe and the utopian socialism of the Saint-Simonians and their ilk. His literary career, despite some brilliant successes, threatened to run aground, whilst those of his competitors and contemporaries sailed serenely on. His abandonment of poetry seems to imply, as P. Viallaneix suggests, an inability to keep pace with the technical virtuosity of Hugo, and the works of the 1830s are almost entirely in prose. His search for consolation led him into the entirely unsuitable arms of Marie Dorval, with whom, despite his mother's admonitions against involvement with actresses, he carried on a tempestuous liaison from 1831. With the death of his mother in 1837 and the final rupture with Marie in 1838, it seems that Vigny's personal life finally fell apart. As Lydia subsided into an inarticulate and adipose middle-age, he amused himself with a series of variously inadequate relationships, whilst in public life, he conducted a series of humiliating campaigns to gain entry to the Académie Française (succeeding only at the sixth attempt in 1845), and twice failed to secure election to the Chambre des Députés after the 1848 Revolution.

Long before his death in 1863 from a particularly painful form of stomach cancer, Vigny appeared to others, and, in one sense, to himself, as a man whom life had passed by: in the eloquent phraseology of M. Toesca, 'son âme s'est trempée à l'eau glacée des échecs' (*25*, p.11). That in itself helps to explain the continuing deep emotional, social, political and metaphysical pessimism of the poetry. Perhaps the key to his isolation can be found in his *Journal*, where he writes: 'Je n'ai jamais pu parvenir à m'intéresser à des imbéciles' (*7*, II, p.1051). Yet the most revealing comment on the man whom Sully-Prudhomme called 'Gentilhomme au front triste et libre, à la frontière / Des vieux âges sombrés et des âges nouveaux' (*16*, p.129) is perhaps that of P. Lasserre, who said of him: 'Il fut jusqu'à la fin celui qui ne veut pas être consolé' (*10*, p.1). For his inability to be consoled *for* the present, we have seen that biographical details can offer some explanation. For his inability to be consoled *by* the present, for his fiercely impenitent belief in the future, it is more particularly in Vigny's peculiar temperament and genius that the explanation can be found.

1. Genesis and Nature of the Collection

Les Destinées, 'la partie la plus brillante de la couronne de Vigny' (*16*, p.77), was not published until after his death. For the last twenty-eight years of his life, after the twin successes of 1835 constituted by the performance of his 'drame' *Chatterton* and the publication of the set of linked stories entitled *Servitude et grandeur militaires*, Vigny's published output was restricted to a handful of poems and an essay on literary copyright, *De Mademoiselle Sedaine et de la propriété littéraire*, all of which appeared in the *Revue des deux mondes* between 1841 and 1844, with the exception of 'La Bouteille à la mer', first published in 1854. These half-dozen poems, together with five more unpublished ones which Vigny left in manuscript, finally appeared in 1864.

Although Vigny had never been an intensely prolific writer, there seems little doubt that the well-springs of his creativity dried up quite dramatically after the mid-1830s. Certainly there were unpublished works over and above the five supplementary poems of *Les Destinées*: a major novel, *Daphné*, written in large measure in 1837 as a sequel to *Stello* (1832), was found among the poet's papers, although it was not finally given to the public until 1912. But had not Vigny written in a letter that 'j'amasse en silence mes écrits nouveaux ... Croiriez-vous que je les ai tellement accumulés que j'ai là, près de moi, une malle entière pleine de romans, d'histoires, de tragédies, de livres de toute forme et de toute nature' (*21*, II, p.157)? Of these no sign. All that has come down to us, apart from some fairly extensive auto-biographical writings, assembled in great part by J. Sangnier under the title *Mémoires inédits*, is the collection of jottings and drafts first released by Ratisbonne in 1867 as the *Journal d'un poète*, and thereafter supplemented by subsequent researchers. Invaluable though this is as a record of Vigny's sentiments and attitudes over a literary career spanning some forty years and more, it seems to confirm that the literary works of his maturity and old age never got beyond the planning stage.

It is not within the purview of this study to try and suggest why Vigny suddenly stopped publishing and writing, as it were in mid-career. Biographical reasons may have played their part — Vigny's mother, to whom he was obsessively attached, died in December 1837, and his extended stop-go love-affair with the actress Marie Dorval finally petered out the following year — but it would surely be simplistic to see these considerations as conclusive, and critics have naturally exercised their ingenuity in seeking alternative solutions. What is certain is that the poet did on a number of occasions sketch out a plan for a new collection of poems, including those he had already published in the *Revue des deux mondes*. It is not, I think, relevant to our considerations here to review these plans in detail, nor to debate how far Vigny may have been committed at one point to the idea of two collections rather than one. The first occasion on which this plan begins to resemble the collection as we have it is in a note headed 'Plan et ordre', dated 4 May 1856; eight of the eleven poems are listed (all except 'Wanda', 'Les Oracles' and 'L'Esprit pur'), interspersed with a series of linking 'rêveries' based on the main themes of the individual poems. (Hence the 'rêverie' on 'La Sauvage' was to deal with 'la civilisation', that on 'La Flûte' with 'l'égalité des âmes', and so forth.) Six years later to the day, Vigny drafted a slightly fuller plan, changing the order of the poems, and including 'Wanda'. This was until recently thought to be his last word on the matter. However, as A. Jarry has shown, there does exist a final plan for a collection entitled *Les Destinées* and sub-titled 'Poèmes philosophiques', drawn up by Vigny on 27 May 1863. This includes all eleven poems in the order in which they were subsequently published by Ratisbonne.

The poems of this collection represent a distillation, effected over a period of twenty-five years (1838-63), of Vigny's philosophy. Ratisbonne published them under the sub-title *Poèmes philosophiques*, although he did not conform to Vigny's wish that the words 'C'était écrit!' should constitute the epigraph of the entire volume (instead he only made it the epigraph of the poem entitled 'Les Destinées'). As usual, Vigny knew what he was doing, and the importance of the words 'C'était écrit!' as an epigraph to the whole volume is a matter to which I shall return. In accordance with the sub-title, it is from the angle of the evolution of Vigny's thought portrayed therein that I shall first discuss these poems. In so doing, I shall clearly have to be selective in my coverage, devoting more attention to some poems than to others, although I think it is important in a collection of this nature, where the poems are both relatively few in number and relatively long (only two contain less than 100 lines), to make some effort to evaluate each one. What I cannot do, given the constraints of space, is to attempt a more detailed coverage peculiar to a critical edition; in consequence I can hardly do more than suggest the extreme thematic density of these poems, and cannot devote to the matter of sources and influences any greater attention than seems to me absolutely necessary for an overall understanding of the poetry. For the contemporary reader, the essential point at issue must be to resolve whether *Les Destinées*, despite their apparently unfinished nature, can be seen to propose a coherent world-view in the form in which they were finally presented to the public.

Despite the variety of themes, styles and dates contained in the collection, I do find it possible to argue that a coherent philosophy emerges from *Les Destinées*, and that the internal contradictions of the collection are more apparent than real. A facile example of such contradictions is the seeming ambivalence of the poet's attitude to nature as expressed in 'La Maison du berger'; more cogent ones might be thought to be the diametrically opposed attitudes to woman as expressed in 'La Colère de Samson' and 'La Maison du berger', or those to civilisation and the social order as expressed in 'La Mort du loup' and 'La Sauvage'; or the incongruity of placing 'Wanda', a denunciation of the savage tyranny of the Czarist regime in Russia, between two such optimistic poems as 'La Bouteille à la mer' and 'L'Esprit pur'. But this collection is no more self-contradictory than any of Vigny's other works: from the beginning of his career his writing offers an intriguing juxtaposition of themes, as I have already suggested in my introductory chapter. What is evident, however, is that the message of hope and optimism which undeniably emerges from *Les Destinées*, and which is confirmed by Vigny's contemporaneous notations in the *Journal*, is far clearer and more persistent than heretofore in his work.

The central theme of the collection, as implied by the title, is that of 'destinée', the oriental goddess of the liminal poem, also entitled 'Les Destinées'. For Vigny, each poem in the cycle represents a facet of actual or realisable human destiny, and the overall tendency of the collection very clearly signifies a movement away from a passively theocentric world-view, as embodied in 'Les Destinées', towards a vibrant celebration of human potential and endeavour, of which 'La Bouteille à la mer' and 'L'Esprit pur' offer respectively a general and a specifically personal manifestation. Formulated more simply, it is a movement away from an old faith to a new. Seen in this light, the ordering of the poems in the collection takes on an internal and developmental coherence, which stresses the theme of *reshaping* man's 'destinée', and which may be summarised, albeit very schematically, as follows. I give in parentheses after each title the probable composition dates of the poems, which, as will be seen, do not always correspond to those indicated by Vigny and printed in subsequent editions of *Les Destinées*.

1. 'Les Destinées' (1849): profound metaphysical pessimism, but containing a residual suggestion of man's collective capacity for resilience against the odds.

2. 'La Maison du berger' (1842-44): social and environmental pessimism, placing much greater stress on human resilience, seen here in predominantly individual and emotional terms (embodied in the figure of the poet and the importance afforded to love).

3. 'Les Oracles' (1862): political pessimism, rejection of political action, and a suggestion in the 'Post-scriptum' of alternative modes of conduct (linking with 'La Maison du berger').

4. 'La Sauvage' (1842): acceptance and celebration of the quintessential values of Western civilisation as a basis for mankind's self-rehabilitation.

5. 'La Colère de Samson' (1839): little can, however, be

expected from human relationships on an individual level.

6. 'La Mort du loup' (1838): one's fellow-men are no more comprehending or supportive as a group than as individuals.

7. 'La Flûte' (1840): solidarity with mankind is nonetheless essential, for it is ultimately here that salvation is to be found.

8. 'Le Mont des oliviers' (1839) and 'Le Silence' (1851): it follows therefore that man must reject the old God of 'Les Destinées' and the values he represents, and become self-reliant.

9. 'La Bouteille à la mer' (1847): he must work for and place his faith in future generations, despite the incomprehension and rejection of his contemporaries.

10. 'Wanda' (1847) and 'Billets' (1857): he must never forget the diabolical lengths to which human savagery can go in impeding his civilising aim.

11. 'L'Esprit pur' (1863): he will triumph, not in his own time, but in the time and in the eyes of future generations.

I must stress that, as it stands, this is only a very generalised and schematic view of *Les Destinées*, which will obviously require modification and elaboration as we consider the poems individually. I also feel it is important to underline once more that the poems do not demonstrate a simple linear development from 'pessimism' to 'optimism': the most we can say is that the chronologically later poems show a greater willingness on Vigny's part to express himself in a more overtly optimistic vein. Ultimately Vigny's world-view is a complex one: it would not be so convincing and moving if it were not.

2. 'Les Destinées' and 'Le Mont des oliviers'

I want first of all to consider the two poems of cosmic pessimism, 'Les Destinées' and 'Le Mont des oliviers'. It is intriguing
to note that in Vigny's 1862 plan for the collection, these two
poems were separated only by 'La Maison du berger', whereas in
the 1863 plan and Ratisbonne's 1864 edition, 'Le Mont des
oliviers' is the eighth poem in the cycle. I think Vigny's purpose
in this respect was to give himself room to make more forcefully
the point about human self-reliance before using 'Le Mont des
oliviers' as a *rappel* of the theme of 'Les Destinées', urging his
readers not to look to God for answers. Be that as it may, and
despite the time-lapse between the composition of the two
poems, they are very closely linked in terms of theme and
meaning. In both, Vigny reaffirms his long-held view of divine
hostility to human happiness and fulfilment, offering us at one
and the same time an audacious variation and a refinement on
the theme. God's accusers in earlier poems had all been human
(or, in the case of Eloa and Satan, representatives of humanity):
Vigny now moves to the logical extreme of that position, and
gives us in 'Le Mont des oliviers' the supreme human angle on
the divine silence by using Christ himself, 'le fils de l'homme'
(MO. 21), to make his points. In this context, the repeated
references to Jesus's *humanity* throughout the poem evidently
have a profound symbolic significance — for example we learn
that in the garden of Gethsemane Jesus 'devint homme' (MO.
27), with a 'cœur mortel' (MO. 28), and 'Eut sur le monde et
l'homme une pensée humaine' (MO. 32). It seems clear that
Vigny had been toying with this theme for some time. Even if we
discount a projected title, 'L'Homme-Dieu', in 1823, the
Journal contains an entry for 11 December 1830, prefiguring his
use of it: 'Le Christ même ne fut-il pas sceptique? — Oui, il le
fut et d'un doute plein d'amour et de pitié pour l'humanité' (*7*,
II, p.924). The logical extension of this view is the section of

thirteen lines that Vigny cut from the finished poem, perhaps less because they were blasphemous (as E. Lauvrière suggests), than because they were confusing — Jesus declares 'Je ne suis pas le fils de Dieu', but implies that the Son of God did in fact exist — 'Hérode a massacré le Sauveur et le roi' — which begs all manner of questions (6, pp.156-57). In 'Les Destinées', on the other hand, the human situation is seen for the first (and last) time from the divine angle, as if Vigny, possessed by a thoroughly British sense of fair play, felt himself under an obligation, at least once, to put God's point of view.

'Les Destinées' evokes a somewhat shadowy and unspecific oriental pre-Christian world ruled over by a predestinarian God to whom Vigny accords the name of Jehovah (D. 51). In this world, which is clearly not intended to be a realistic representation of that of the Old Testament Jews (no deities similar to the 'destinées' exist in Jewish theology), but rather to depict a general pre-Christian world-state, the 'destinées', emissaries of Jehovah, hold absolute sway:

> Depuis le premier jour de la création,
> Les pieds lourds et puissants de chaque Destinée
> Pesaient sur chaque tête et sur toute action. (D. 1-3)

Mankind is first compared to a team of oxen (D. 5), subject to the supreme authority, the 'joug de plomb' of these 'froides déités' (D. 7), and then to a people of 'esclaves' (D. 8), similarly subservient to these 'Tristes divinités du monde oriental' (D. 13). This state of affairs subsists from time immemorial until

> Un soir, il arriva que l'antique planète
> Secoua sa poussière. — Il se fit un grand cri:
> 'Le Sauveur est venu, voici le jeune athlète,
>
> Il a le front sanglant et le côté meurtri,
> Mais la Fatalité meurt au pied du Prophète,
> La Croix monte et s'étend sur nous comme un abri!'
> (D. 22-27)

The coming of Christ (nowhere in this poem referred to as the Son of God, it may be noted) is thus here perceived by humanity as a turning-point in its fortunes, the destruction of the 'destinées' and the 'fatalité' they represent by Jesus, mankind's supreme embodiment, to enable man to create for himself a new 'destinée', based not on a predestinarian God, but on his own free will — 'la Fatalité meurt au pied du Prophète'. This same point is made by Jesus himself in 'Le Mont des oliviers': his coming has effected a division in time — 'j'ai coupé les temps en deux parts, l'une esclave / Et l'autre libre' (MO. 55-56) — and it is significant that in both poems the word 'esclave' is used to describe mankind's pre-Christian state. Christ's appeal to God to allow him to explain to mankind the paradoxes of earthly existence (MO. 87-130) has as its avowed objective to 'faire ouvrir l'ongle aux Peines Eternelles, / Lâcher leur proie humaine et reployer leurs ailes' (MO. 127-28), and finds its exact parallels in 'Les Destinées', where the goddesses are evoked as 'un vol de vautours' (D. 16), controlling mankind with an 'ongle sans pitié' (D. 19), and ultimately returning to Heaven in a flight 'sans ailes' (D. 40), before resuming their reign over their 'proie éternelle' (D. 94). As Christ intercedes with the God he calls 'Mon Père' (MO. 12), and underlines his wish to leave 'sur ce globe incomplet / Dont le gémissement sans repos m'appelait' (MO. 77-78) two angels, 'La Certitude heureuse et l'Espoir confiant' (MO. 81), relieving man of the need to doubt or despair, so we find in 'Les Destinées' the cosmic backcloth to this essentially human drama:

> Tous les astres émus restèrent en silence,
> Attendant avec l'Homme, en la même stupeur,
> Le suprême décret de la Toute-Puissance. (D. 46-48)

The drama of the cosmos is mentioned only in passing in 'Le Mont des oliviers', where the focus is essentially, as I have suggested, on the human, rather than the divine, angle:

> Et la Terre trembla, sentant la pesanteur
> Du Sauveur qui tombait aux pieds du créateur.

> (MO. 33-34)

It is at this point that the irony of the diptych-like construction
of the two poems achieves its full significance. As Jesus pleads
for mankind and the continuation of his own mission (MO.
35-36), the 'destinées' group themselves round Jehovah (D. 51)
to plead for themselves. Thus the Almighty is at the same time
listening to two diametrically opposed perceptions of man's own
'destinée'. Just as the 'destinées' ask of God 'la Loi de l'avenir'
(D. 55), so Jesus begs that his blood may be used 'pour laver
l'avenir' (MO. 58). Whereas Jesus sees God as (potentially) a
'Père Libérateur' (MO. 59), the 'destinées' envisage him as the
creator of 'le grand piège du Sort' (D. 61). And it is they who are
proved right: the God addressed by both sets of plaintiffs is
indeed a hostile God, the God of the Old Testament rather than
the New. The outcome of the unequal confrontation is not in
doubt. In 'Le Mont des oliviers', no answer is forthcoming —
has God actually listened at all?:

> Ainsi le divin fils parlait au divin Père.
> Il se prosterne encore, il attend, il espère,
> Mais il renonce. (MO. 131-33)

On the divine side of the equation, things are rather different.
Here too, there is a pause before judgement (D. 76-78), but the
silence is not, as in man's case, permanent. Here, for the first
(and last) time in Vigny's poetry, God speaks. But he does not
speak to Jesus, nor, by extension, to mankind, and his purpose
is to confirm man's condemnation. In a grim parody of Christ's
baptism, underlining in Vigny's eyes its quintessential purpose-
lessness in terms of the redemption it purported to bring,

> Une voix descendit, venant de ces hauteurs
> Où s'engendrent sans fin les mondes dans l'espace;
> Cette voix, de la terre emplit les profondeurs (D. 79-81)

The voice of God announces the continuation of the old order:

> 'Retournez en mon nom, Reines, je suis la Grâce.
> L'Homme sera toujours un nageur incertain

Dans les ondes du temps qui se mesure et passe'.

(D. 82-84)[1]

The Almighty is as tenacious as ever of the secrets of existence. Man's destiny, his 'loi perpétuelle' (D. 92), according to God must be: 'Faire ce que je veux pour venir OÙ JE SAIS' (D. 93). As the chorus of 'destinées' returns 'vers sa proie éternelle / Afin d'y ressaisir sa domination' (D. 94-95), in the garden of Gethsemane the answer to Jesus's prayer is vouchsafed in a less explicit, but no less final way — 'la torche de Judas' (MO. 142), the harbinger of betrayal and death, is seen in the trees. As, implicitly, the 'destinées' return to earth, the closing lines of 'Le Mont des oliviers' signal the reimposition of their rule:

> La Terre sans clartés, sans astre et sans aurore,
> Et sans clartés de l'âme ainsi qu'elle est encore,
> Frémissait. (MO. 139-41)

The final 'septain' of 'Le Mont des oliviers', entitled 'Le Silence', is dated 2 April 1862, although it seems probable that it had been written long before and that Vigny's fictitious dating is designed to stress the persistence of the view it puts forward. Its basic point is that the failure of Jesus's intercession, the refusal of God to break his silence, leaves humankind 'comme un monde avorté' (MO. 146) (cf. 'la race timide, incomplète et rebelle' (D. 96)), and that humanity must accept and act upon the logical consequences of this:

> Le juste opposera le dédain à l'absence
> Et ne répondra plus que par un froid silence
> Au silence éternel de la Divinité. (MO. 146-48)

---

[1] All four gospels recount the baptism of Jesus by John, after which 'Jesus ... went up straightway out of the water: and, lo, the heavens were opened unto him, and he saw the Spirit of God descending like a dove, and lighting upon him: and, lo, a voice from heaven, saying, This is my beloved Son, in whom I am well pleased' (*Matthew*, 4, 16-17). The point here is that the 'destinées' descend like the dove, but instead of man's liberation from the elements (an important aspect of the old world for Vigny: see below, p.64), the effect is to consign him to their eternal thrall: 'L'homme sera toujours un nageur incertain / Dans les ondes du temps qui se mesure et passe' (D. 83-84). For Vigny's re-use of this image in terms of man's ultimate liberation, see below, p.75.

It is a trifle paradoxical that a poem so fundamentally concerned with human endeavour should seem to end in what is effectively a philosophical impasse, and in a sense I would be inclined to read into this stanza an implied Voltairian adjuration to cultivate our garden. It is noticeable in this respect that 'Les Destinées', after the return of the 'destinées' to earth, shifts its focus from the cosmic to the human plane. This, I think, suggests the way Vigny's mind is running. Despite Jesus's failure, things *have* changed: mankind is stronger and can begin, though still 'en deuil', to fight back:

Mais, plus forte à présent, dans ce sombre duel,
Notre âme en deuil combat ces Esprits impassibles.

(D. 101-02)

The word 'âme', it will be seen, is a *leitmotiv*, one of the keywords of *Les Destinées*. It is the source of human resilience, the kernel of the effort to build a new world and a new 'destinée'. As God betrays his creation in these two linked poems, we find in both of them the concept of the 'âme' in darkness (MO. 140; D. 102, both quoted above). Into that darkness will come light, not the false light of Judas's torch, but real illumination. It is our responsibility as human beings to participate in the battle for that illumination. The stanza 'Le Silence' reflects Vigny's disillusionment in the final analysis with Jesus who, he seems to suggest, though in many ways a pattern and example, ultimately fails because

[...] il renonce et dit: 'Que votre Volonté
Soit faite et non la mienne et pour l'Eternité!'

(MO. 133-34)

I want to be quite clear here that Vigny does not spurn Jesus completely. The *Journal* is full of statements to the contrary, perhaps best summarised by an entry of 1829 in which Vigny wrote that 'l'humanité devrait tomber à genoux devant cette histoire, parce que le sacrifice est ce qu'il y a de plus beau au monde, et qu'un Dieu né sur la crèche et mort sur la croix dépasse les bornes des plus grands sacrifices' (*7*, II, p.890). But in this instance Vigny believes that Jesus's renunciation was wrong. It is quite simply unconditional surrender. Jesus *gives up*. He is led away — the image is appropriate — like a lamb to the slaughter. He *accepts* his failure. This is the distinction between Jesus and 'le juste' in 'Le Silence'. The latter, by his defiant silence, implies that God no longer figures for him in the equation of life, and that our attention must now be devoted to building a new life without him. Or, as Vigny writes in his *Journal* in 1843:

> Jésus, Notre Seigneur, fils de l'homme, a pris sur lui, mais en vain, de demander la lumière et la certitude à Dieu. Si Dieu l'a refusée à celui qui nous représente par ses souffrances et sa croix, notre devoir est de nous résigner au doute, mais de nous entr'aider ... Que les hommes se rapprochent donc; qu'ils laissent à jamais le soin inutile des philosophies, et renoncent à pénétrer un ciel toujours voilé. (*7*, II, p.1203).

The verb 'renoncer' recurs here, but in a different context: it is not the struggle that has to be given up, as Jesus does, but any attempt to understand a God who, as 'Les Destinées' retrospectively proves (if further proof were needed) must irrefutably be seen as hostile. A draft for a poem entitled 'La Herse' (1843) similarly stigmatises 'l'inertie de Dieu' refusing to instruct man in 'le mot de l'énigme de la Création' (*7*, II, p.1204).

It is the extreme difficulty of building this new life that is illustrated in the last eight tercets of 'Les Destinées'. The change of focus symbolises for Vigny the new road mankind must travel once freed of the constraints imposed by the old religions. In this respect it is perhaps Jesus as an individual rather than Christianity as a creed which offers the glimpse of hope. If, in the last tercet, Vigny can essentially imply that all religions are much the same, and all equally oppressive —

Notre mot éternel est-il: C'ETAIT ECRIT?
— SUR LE LIVRE DE DIEU, dit l'Orient esclave;

Et l'Occident répond: — SUR LE LIVRE DU CHRIST.

(D. 121-23)

and can write in his *Journal* (1834) that 'la religion du Christ est une religion de désespoir, puisqu'il désespère de la vie' (*7*, II, p.1015), nonetheless the example of Jesus has perhaps fired, or can fire, mankind with a belief in its own potential irrespective of religious dogma. In 'Le Mont des oliviers' Jesus himself largely repudiates the religion that will be instituted in his name (MO. 63-66). The impossibility of mankind wriggling free of such stultifying metaphysical conditioning seems almost absolute, yet this peak can be scaled: as Vigny notes in his *Journal*, 'le fort fait ses événements, le faible subit ceux que la destinée lui impose' (*7*, II, p.880). It is the 'fort' whom Vigny has in mind in the following tercets of 'Les Destinées':

Arbitre libre et fier des actes de sa vie,
Si notre cœur s'entr'ouvre au parfum des vertus,
S'il s'embrase à l'amour, s'il s'élève au génie,

Que l'ombre des Destins, Seigneur, n'oppose plus
A nos belles ardeurs une immuable entrave,
A nos efforts sans fin des coups inattendus! (D. 112-17)

This appeal, directed to the 'Dieu juste' (D. 111), is fundamentally, I think, an appeal not to a transformed Jehovah (the leopard does not change his spots), but to a new God. Ultimately, however, since this God, as we shall see, is essentially a divinisation of all that is best in man (hence supremely anthropomorphic), the appeal is logically pointless — man must work out his own salvation. In the meantime, Vigny can at least console himself with a fantasy about the Day of Judgment which will see a distinctly 'poetic' justice meted out to the Divine Oppressor:

Ce sera ce jour-là que Dieu viendra se justifier devant toutes les âmes et tout ce qui est vie. Il paraîtra et parlera, il dira clairement pourquoi la création et pourquoi la souffrance et la mort de l'innocence, etc. En ce moment, ce sera le genre humain ressuscité qui sera le juge, et l'Eternel, le Créateur, sera jugé par les générations rendues à la vie. (*7*, II, p.1377)

3. 'La Colère de Samson' and 'La Mort du loup'

I now wish to look at two of the more specifically personal poems in the collection. This is not to say that either 'Le Mont des oliviers' or 'Les Destinées' is devoid of subjectivity, and in the case of the former I would argue that there are, and must be, distinct analogies between the figure of Christ and that of the poet, analogies that will become even more evident in 'La Bouteille à la mer'. But if, in these two poems, it can indisputably be argued that Vigny *is* speaking, not just for himself, but for all mankind, in the pair of poems I now want to consider — 'La Colère de Samson' and 'La Mort du loup' — the inspiration strikes me as undoubtedly much more personal, albeit not devoid of universal application. Indeed, it would be difficult to dispute the opinion that 'La Colère de Samson' is the most intimately personal poem Vigny ever wrote.

In the imperfect world characterised by 'Les Destinées' and 'Le Mont des oliviers', the most profound alienation and suffering is that experienced by the hypersensitive poet or individual (in this context we may see ourselves, the reader, as an extension/universalisation of Vigny's victimisation theme). As we have already understood from the non-communication between Christ and his disciples in 'Le Mont des oliviers' (MO. 17-20), mankind as a species is not only alienated from God, but unreceptive to the suffering of his fellow-man. This definition by no means excludes woman, as Vigny in 'La Colère de Samson' takes it upon himself to tell us. These two poems are poems of social and sentimental despair. Both Samson and the wolf die alone and betrayed.

Both the poems were written shortly after the time of Vigny's greatest personal crisis (1837-38), which partly explains their lugubrious tone. Samson takes for granted the battle against religious conditioning (the non-interventionism of the Almighty is referred to in line 36 and again in line 105), and characterises

life as a divinely-ordained struggle for survival against the odds
(CS. 53-56). Man is dependent on woman and her love —
'L'Homme a toujours besoin de caresse et d'amour' (CS. 39) —
yet it is here in his intimate relationships far more than in the
daily struggle for life that he is betrayed:

> Mais il n'a pas encor fini toute sa tâche. —
> Vient un autre combat plus secret, traître et lâche;
> Sous son bras, sous son cœur se livre celui-là,
> Et, plus ou moins, la Femme est toujours DALILA.
>   (CS. 57-60)

For Vigny, 'puissamment organisé pour la volupté physique' (*7*,
II, p.980), woman had to be both maternal and submissive
(points which will emerge in the depiction of the ideal woman in
'La Maison du berger'). Marie Dorval quite evidently did not
fulfil these requirements, and is accused in consequence, not
only of calculating frigidity (CS. 61), but also, somewhat
implausibly, of lesbianism (or such is the interpretation that
P.-G. Castex places on lines 62-67). The failure of the ideal is
underlined by the following lines, given to Samson:

> — Donc ce que j'ai voulu, Seigneur, n'existe pas. —
> Celle à qui va l'amour et de qui vient la vie,
> Celle-là, par Orgueil, se fait notre ennemie. (CS. 72-74)

It could well be argued that Vigny's resentment against woman's
failure in her maternal role had been exacerbated by his
mother's recent death. Whatever the truth of the matter, this
emotional bankruptcy of woman leads to Samson's destruction
— 'mon âme / N'avait pour aliment que l'amour d'une femme'
(CS. 81-82) — the only consolation being that, in his downfall,
he destroys his perfidious (and now remorseful) betrayer.

Whatever the rights and wrongs of the Vigny-Marie Dorval
relationship, it is clear that Vigny had cast the actress in a role
for which she was eminently unsuited. The child-woman was
also to be a Muse. 'Ce sont les peines de l'âme que celles que
donnent les Dalila' (*8*, p.429), wrote Vigny; and, more explicitly:

L'Amour physique et seulement physique pardonne toute infidélité. L'Amant sait ou croit qu'il ne retrouvera nulle volupté pareille ailleurs et, tout en gémissant, s'en repaît. Mais toi, Amour de l'âme, Amour passionné, tu ne peux rien pardonner. (7, II, p.973).

We note here the recurrence of the theme of the 'âme', the source of human resilience, in the context of love, marking the transition to 'La Maison du berger', where the only worthwhile relationship is shown to be at one and the same time physical *and* spiritual, a complete blending of body and soul, succinctly prefigured by the description in the novel *Daphné* (1837) of the nun Héloïse awaiting her priest-lover Abelard:

O profanations involontaires! mélanges ineffables de l'Amour, de la Sainteté et de la Science que personne encore n'a compris entièrement! Soupirs mystiques et passionnés d'un amour énergique et pieux à la fois! Doubles Extases des âmes et des jeunes corps enflammés d'amour! (7, II, p.783)

On the surface a similarly negative message emerges from 'La Mort du loup'. This poem has always given rise to a certain amount of hilarity amongst critics because of the obvious anthropomorphism of the imagery. Self-evidently, however, Vigny is not concerned to provide us with an authentic narration of a wolf-hunt, and it seems idle to pick out inconsistencies, the more so as the event recounted is clearly, as F. Germain observes (*17*, p.68), a transposition of the capture of the Russian encampment in 'La Canne de jonc' (*Servitude et grandeur militaires*). Vigny's purpose is to use the wolf as a symbol of man, more specifically the gifted individual, in society. Intriguingly the poem offers a twin focus. We are indeed asked to see the wolf as the representative of the poet hounded by society, and in this respect the poem has close links with two of Vigny's major works of the earlier 1830s, the novel *Stello* and the 'drame' *Chatterton*, which also deal with the theme of society's hostility to the poet. But Vigny is also present in human form in the poem in the guise of the first-person narrator. 'Je' is a participant in the hunt and the kill of the wolf — Vigny speaks of

> [...] *nos* coups de feu qui traversaient sa chair
> Et *nos* couteaux aigus qui, comme des tenailles,
> Se croisaient en plongeant dans ses larges entrailles.
>
> (ML. 48-50; my italics)

The reference in line 61 to 'mon fusil sans poudre' even indicates that the narrator has shot the wolf. But he then holds back, unable to resolve himself after the wolf's death, 'à poursuivre sa Louve' (ML. 63), and in a sense merges himself with the dead wolf in the final section of the poem:

> — Ah! je t'ai bien compris, sauvage voyageur,
> Et ton dernier regard m'est allé jusqu'au cœur!
>
> (ML. 79-80)

The implication seems to be that (in the words of Hegel quoted by Simone de Beauvoir as an epigraph to *L'Invitée*), 'Chaque conscience poursuit la mort de l'autre': we are each, at one and the same time, victims in our own right, and victimisers of others — man, quite literally, is a wolf to man! In the latter category, however, there is a chance for us to learn the error of our ways — if 'je' participates in the killing of the wolf, the revulsion he experiences, together with the wolf's example in death, causes him to hold back from the butchery of the she-wolf and the cubs. In the former category, our perspectives are limited, but real enough. The wolf instructs us:

> [...] Si tu peux, fais que ton âme arrive,
> A force de rester studieuse et pensive,
> Jusqu'à ce haut degré de stoïque fierté
> Où, naissant dans les bois, j'ai tout d'abord monté.
>
> Gémir, pleurer, prier est également lâche.
> — Fais énergiquement ta longue et lourde tâche,
> Dans la voie où le Sort a voulu t'appeler,

Puis après, comme moi, souffre et meurs sans parler.

(ML. 81-88)

A number of Vigny's essential themes emerge here. We find a further reference to the 'âme' as the source of human greatness, which, 'studieuse et pensive', will give him the strength to resist 'the slings and arrows of outrageous fortune', whilst the 'stoïque fierté' represents here, no less than in *Servitude et grandeur militaires*, the most meaningful way of confronting a hostile world. It is significant, moreover, that the wolf's advice precludes any recourse to God ('prier' is as 'lâche' as 'gémir' or 'pleurer'), and similarly any recourse to suicide (Vigny had been much criticised for the suicide of the hero in *Chatterton*). The wolf's advice is 'Fais énergiquement ta longue et lourde tâche'. That task will change in nature and emphasis over the years: in 1839 it is seemingly a question of living (difficult enough, in Vigny's view) to the best possible effect.

Yet that is not all. Despite being hedged about by doom and disaster it is incumbent upon us to make something of our lives through the medium of this 'stoïque fierté'. In 1832, Vigny wrote in his *Journal*: 'L'espérance rend lâche. La certitude d'un destin irrévocable rend courageux' (*7*, II, p.957). When at one juncture he contemplated introducing each poem by a 'récitatif' (his own term), he wrote for 'La Mort du loup': 'La vie est triste et l'éternité douteuse. Mais l'homme, s'il voulait seulement voir près de lui, puiserait partout la force de supporter la vie et de lutter contre elle' (*18*, p.81). This interpretation of the poem would seem to derive confirmation from the letter that Vigny wrote about it to Camilla Maunoir on 31 January 1843: 'Considérez la France actuelle, depuis dix ans, et dites-moi si j'ai eu tort de lui présenter un cordial et de lui dire *Surge*' (*3*, p.123; the italicised word is the imperative of the Latin *surgere*, 'to arise'). In this context I think it is undeniably an error to see the poem as an indictment of the values of civilised society. Certainly the she-wolf saves the cubs

[...] afin

De pouvoir leur apprendre à bien souffrir la faim,

A ne jamais entrer dans le pacte des villes
Que l'homme a fait avec les animaux serviles

(ML. 67-70)

But this is surely more a condemnation of human attitudes than
the values of civilised society. The difference between the
message of 'La Mort du loup' and that of 'La Sauvage', so
frequently remarked upon, resides in this distinction. Pope once
observed that the ninth beatitude was 'Blessed is the man who
expects nothing, for he shall never be disappointed', a reflection
on the actual behaviour of man in society, not on the values
which are the moral guides of that society. It may be added that,
as P.-G. Castex remarks, 'La Mort du loup' is 'un poème conçu
au lendemain d'une crise et Vigny ne s'est pas tenu à la position
extrême qu'il paraissait y défendre' (*4*, p.134).

4. 'Wanda', 'Les Oracles', 'La Maison du berger'

The next three poems are all germane to Vigny's political views, in which respect they maintain the pessimism of the previous poems, although two of them do allow us to glimpse Vigny's prospective exit from the impasse. They include what is probably Vigny's most important and possibly his best-known poem, 'La Maison du berger', and two less celebrated compositions, 'Wanda' (in my view rather unjustly neglected) and 'Les Oracles' (perhaps rather more justly so). 'Les Oracles' has an extended 'Post-scriptum', which will be more relevantly considered in the context of 'La Maison du berger'.

'Wanda' and 'Les Oracles' constitute what can only be described as a blistering attack on specific forms of political regime. 'Wanda' savages absolutist tyranny (in the event that of Russia), whereas in 'Les Oracles' Vigny turns his attention to Western European democracy. It is difficult (and in any case irrelevant) to say which of the two comes off better from Vigny's diatribes: as evidenced by works earlier in his career (not only poems like 'Le Trappiste' but prose works such as *Stello*) Vigny had no time for any of the currently constituted forms of government.[2] He noted in his *Journal* that 'le monde a la démarche d'un sot, il s'avance en se balançant mollement entre deux absurdités: le droit divin et la souveraineté du peuple' (*7*, II, p.930). 'Wanda' is in essence an extended meditation on an observation of 1824: 'Rien de plus *immoral* que la *force* et le pouvoir absolu qui est la force' (*7*, II, p.881). The basis of this moving narrative poem is a true story deriving from a meeting in 1845 between Vigny (the 'Français' of the poem) and Wanda Kossakowskaya, although the material used for the depiction of

[2] It should be noted, however, that Vigny always excluded the United States of America from these strictures. In 1835 he noted in his *Journal*: 'Le seul gouvernement dont à présent l'idée ne me soit pas intolérable, c'est celui d'une république dont la constitution serait pareille à celle des Etats-Unis américains' (*7*, II, p.1021). In this context it is clearly significant that he selected America as the setting for his poem on the theme of civilisation, 'La Sauvage'.

life in Siberia is mainly drawn from the marquis de Custine's book *La Russie en 1839* (1843), which echoed Vigny's own views on the role of the aristocracy in the state. The central figure in the narration is Wanda's sister, Princess Trubetskoi, who had insisted on accompanying her husband into internal exile in Siberia after the failure of the Decembrists' rising against Czar Nicholas I in 1825. This revolt is interpreted by Vigny, a staunch advocate of the political principles of Montesquieu, as an attempt by the aristocracy to resume its rightful role of mediator between monarch and people. Significantly, however, it is seen only in retrospect, emphasising its pointlessness (and by extension the pointlessness of all political action). It is Princess Trubetskoi, speaking to Wanda, who argues this:

> L'Empereur tout-puissant, qui voit d'en haut les choses,
> Du Prince mon Seigneur voulut faire un forçat.
> Dieu seul peut réviser un jour ces grandes causes
> Entre le souverain, le sujet et l'État. (W. 29-32)

Politics, therefore, is not a human, but a divine field of action — 'Dieu *seul* peut réviser un jour ces grandes causes' — and, knowing what we know of God in Vigny's work, there is no specific reason to hope or expect justice, as interpreted in human terms, to be done. Nonetheless, Vigny confers an epic grandeur on the struggle between the monarchy and the nobility (W. 108-12): in his eyes, as we have already seen, an action does not require a positive result to possess an intrinsic beauty in itself. The poem is on one level a glorification of the fruitless heroism of the Decembrists, and more especially the equivalent heroism of the princess, one of those 'Éponines du Nord' (W. 103), who, submissive and maternal — Vigny's ideal woman — sacrifices herself to accompany her husband to the mines of Siberia, in a bleak parody of the Poet-Eva relationship in 'La Maison du berger'. But its real focus is elsewhere. It is here that we begin to see the shift in emphasis in Vigny's thinking. The most fundamental source of the Czar's guilt is not the physical tyranny he exercises over Prince Trubetskoi (representing the failed rebels), but the mental tyranny exerted over the children of the prince's marriage. In the twenty years of exile, or, as Vigny more accurately defines it, 'vingt hivers' (W. 60), we learn that 'Quatre enfants ont grandi dans l'ombre des caveaux' (W. 63). (Vigny omitted, doubtless as rather too heavy-handedly didactic, a detail, found in his prose draft, referring to the princess: 'Dieu n'a fécondé son sein que lorsqu'il a été sanctifié par le dévouement' (*18*, p.73).) The mother's wish is that they be taught to read, since they are princes, 'Et n'ont rien fait encor qui blesse l'Empereur' (W. 70). This request is relayed to the Czar:

> Après dix ans d'attente il répondit enfin:
> 'Un esclave a besoin d'un marteau, non d'un livre:
> La lecture est fatale à ceux-là qui, pour vivre,
> Doivent avoir bon bras pour gagner un bon pain'.
> (W. 74-77)

In that simple statement of the time-span elapsing between request and response, as in the earlier description of the Czar as 'toujours affable et clément souverain' (W. 72), there is a bitterness of irony reminiscent of Voltaire's famous description of war in chapter III of *Candide*. The Czar's refusal to grant the mother's request, a refusal of which the enormity is character-ised by her tearless reaction — 'Ses yeux secs sont glacés d'épouvante et d'horreur!' (W. 84) — is a crime against the spirit — the 'âme' — for it denies mankind in its future generations the only weapon it possesses by which it can hope to rise superior to its physical servitude, the old order as current-ly constituted. Vigny formulates this point, albeit rather gnomically, in the first stanza of 'le Français''s reply:

> Wanda, j'écoute encore après votre silence ...
> J'ai senti sur mon cœur poser ce doigt d'airain
> Qui porte au bout du monde à toute âme qui pense
> Les épouvantements du fatal souverain.
> Cet homme enseveli vivant avec sa femme,
> Ces esclaves enfants dont on va tuer l'âme,
> Est-ce de notre siècle ou du temps d'Ugolin? (W. 85-91)

Now the 'doigt d'airain' is quite clearly that of the 'destinées' (D. 11), of whom the Czar, 'fatal souverain', and his regime, thus clearly become a physical manifestation. Equally significant, however, is the repetition of the noun 'âme' in this stanza. 'Toute âme qui pense' is able to perceive 'Les épouvantements du fatal souverain', perception implying distancing and an embryonic capacity to resist and eventually to overcome. But the princess's children are 'esclaves' (another keyword from 'Les Destinées') and their 'âme' will be destroyed by the refusal to permit them to learn to read, which takes on a universal symbolic connotation. To deprive man of the capacity for mental resilience is to deprive him of what, in Vigny's view, makes him fundamentally human and gives him the power to resist an imposed 'destinée' and to create his own. In this context, the children of the princess are twice assimilated to 'agneaux', betrayed by the 'mauvais pasteur' (W. 66-67) and failing to achieve redemption by their innocence — the Czar does *not* say: 'Le brebis m'a vaincu par le sang des agneaux' (W. 161). Both these references obviously have Biblical connotations, and Vigny's point is further underlined by the description of the dead princess as 'la sainte' and 'la femme forte' (W. 171): the children and their mother are both martyrs for the new faith and victims of the old order. As if to underline how little can be expected of so nauseous a regime, Vigny, in the guise of 'le Français', ceases to adopt a narrative style in stanza XXIV (the last of his interposition, and of the original poem), and moves into a prophetic vein: the Czar's silence, parallel, no doubt, to that of the God whose vicegerent on earth he theoretically is, will persist:

> Mais il n'a point parlé, mais cette année encore
> Heure par heure en vain lentement tombera,
> Et la neige sans bruit, sur la terre incolore
> Aux pieds des exilés nuit et jour gèlera.
> Silencieux devant son armée en silence
> Le Czar, en mesurant la cuirasse et la lance,
> Passera sa revue et toujours se taira. (W. 162-68)

Wanda's 'second billet', however, dated from the time of the Crimean war, eight years after the poem's original composition, suggests a desire on Vigny's part to offer a more hopeful conclusion. The fall of Sebastopol is seen as divine retribution on the Czar, who is 'mort de rage' (W. 178) at the news. Western civilisation, in the patriotic shape of 'l'aigle de France' (W. 176), has destroyed this symbol of the Czar's power, and 'On dit que la balance immense / Du Seigneur a paru quand la foudre a tonné' (W. 178-79). We may well ask ourselves what the Divinity is up to here. M. Cambien suggests that 'Dieu, il est vrai ... punit l'autocrate en frappant "au cœur de l'ours" (W. 175). Mais le "Second billet de Wanda" précise que c'est du fait de "l'aigle de France" que "la foudre a tonné". La divinité continue donc ici à jouer les utilités' (13, p.118). I am not sure, though, that I find this interpretation very convincing, because it seems rather bewildering and contradictory, in view of what we know of God in Vigny's work. I would argue that this intervention is not that of the old God of 'Les Destinées' undergoing what can only be interpreted as a sudden change of heart, but, as we shall see from a similar occurrence in 'Les Oracles', that of the new God, the 'Dieu des idées' of 'La Bouteille à la mer'. Forgiveness, however, is not granted to the dead Czar, for, as Vigny implies, all things can be forgiven save one, the crime perpetrated against the spirit:

L'Épouse, la Martyre, a peut-être fait grâce,
Dieu du ciel! — Mais la mère a-t-elle pardonné?
(W. 181-82)

I think we can safely assume that the rejection of the princess's petition constitutes, in Vigny's new secularised theology, the 'blasphemy against the Holy Ghost' which 'shall not be forgiven unto men'. This point becomes clearer in the context of 'L'Esprit pur', and I shall return to it.

To the castigation of absolutist tyranny and its unforgivable crimes in 'Wanda' corresponds the castigation of democratic egalitarianism in 'Les Oracles'. Modern readers are liable to find this difficult and allusive poem rather heavy going, overloaded as it is with references to the contemporary political situation. Fundamentally, what Vigny is attacking in his rather obscure and wordy way, are the inadequacies of the bourgeois monarchy of Louis-Philippe (whom he calls 'Ulysse' in the poem), and explaining the reasons for its failure. The lessons of previous monarchical disasters are of no avail: despite all his apparent wisdom and experience (whence the sobriquet), Louis-Philippe is swept away in 1848 by a revolution completed in a mere three hours, whereas at least the revolution of 1830 which disposed of Charles X took a more seemly three days:

> Ulysse avait connu les hommes et les villes,
> Sondé le lac de sang des Révolutions,
> Des Saints et des Héros les cœurs faux et serviles,
> Et le sable mouvant des Constitutions.
> — Et pourtant, un matin, des royales demeures,
> Comme un autre en trois jours, il tombait en trois heures,
> Sous le vent empesté des Déclamations. (O. 22-28)

The Parliamentarism of the Orleans monarchy was a talking-shop, 'full of sound and fury, / Signifying nothing', as the rather laboured reference to *Hamlet* in stanza VI implies. The 1848 Revolutionaries are certainly no better — 'le vent empesté des Déclamations' led Vigny in his fear of public disorder to support Louis-Napoléon Bonaparte (though not, it seems, before he had sought and failed to acquire the post of ambassador to London from Lamartine's provisional government). Admittedly Vigny always maintained that he believed in democracy, but the form of parliamentary regime perpetuated by the Orleans monarchy was anathema to him, for the same reasons as the Bourbon Restoration had ultimately become anathema to Lamartine — indeed there are considerable similarities between the two poets' excoriations of these defunct regimes.[3] Democracy, for Vigny, is a basis on which to build, a

[3] In particular, the image of the desert is found in 'Les Révolutions', with the same connotation as in 'Les Oracles'. Lamartine's message is that man must move on out of the desert, but that politicians insist on immobility, repairing the crumbling political institutions of the past — 'En vain le Temps, qui rit de vos Babels, les broie ... / Vous les rebâtissez toujours, toujours de même'.

desert from which an oasis must be created (O. 66-67), but the opportunity to be constructive has been sacrificed to feuding and infighting (O. 71-72), and for Vigny, such conduct, 'Traçant de faux Devoirs et frappant de vrais Droits' (O. 81), seems just as culpable as that of the Czar in 'Wanda', for he is just as unforgiving. The scales that judge the Czar in 'Wanda' now make a second appearance, this time overtly representing the new order, to judge the demagogues:

> Reines de mes pensées! ô Raison! ô Justice!
> Vous avez déployé vos balances d'acier
> Pour peser ces Esprits d'audace et d'artifice
> Que le Destin venait enfin d'humilier. (O. 50-53)

And when Vigny rhetorically urges himself, in the 'Post-scriptum', at a time when, it appears, twelve years have passed (O. 94): 'Oublions et la Faute et la Fuite et le Sang' (O. 95), the answer is

> — Non. Dans l'Histoire il est de noirs anniversaires
> Dont le spectre revient pour troubler le Présent.
>
> (O. 97-98)[4]

The reason for this harshness is ultimately very similar to that which Vigny adduces to justify his stance against the Czar in 'Wanda':

> S'agiter et blesser est l'instinct des vipères;
> L'Homme ainsi contre l'Homme a son instinct fatal;
> Il retourne ses dards et nourrit ses colères
> Au réservoir caché de son poison natal.

Interestingly, Lamartine also uses the image of mankind that will later recur in Vigny's 'Les Destinées', that of the beast of burden, 'le bœuf à courte haleine', stressing in a similar way the need for man's liberation. See A. de Lamartine, *Œuvres poétiques complètes* (Paris, Pléiade, 1963), pp.510-19.

[4] The composition date of 'Les Oracles' is generally accepted to be 1862, which means that Vigny's mathematics are at fault: fourteen years, not twelve, had passed since the 1848 Revolution. M. Tournier seems to be alone in making a case for the poem having been written in 1850 (*6*, p.66).

Dans quelque cercle obscur qu'on les ait vus descendre,
Homme ou serpent, blottis sous le verre ou la cendre,
Mordront le diamant ou mordront le cristal. (O. 106-12)

The convoluted imagery can only be understood if, as V.-L.
Saulnier points out, the words 'vipère' and 'serpent' are understood to mean 'scorpion'. Such a reading again underlines the
parallel with 'Wanda' — the Parliamentarians cannot be forgiven because they have turned their venom against their own
kind, humanity, endeavouring to destroy what is best in man,
i.e., 'le diamant' or 'le cristal'.

With the terms 'diamant' and 'cristal', we enter an area of
extreme density of imagery, and the parallels between the 'Post-
scriptum' of 'Les Oracles' and seminal sections of 'La Maison
du berger' are so close that it will be more helpful to deal with
them both together. Let us therefore move on to an analysis of
the latter poem, the meaning of which is central to Vigny's entire
poetic output.

'La Maison du berger' is dedicated, as is 'L'Esprit pur' and,
by implication, 'Les Oracles' (see lines 1-3), to 'Eva'. Critics
have derived much entertainment from the activity of Eva-
spotting, but it now seems established that the original model for
the portrait in 'La Maison du berger' was the Irishwoman
Tryphina Holmes.[5] I am in any case inclined to view this contro-
versy as 'un faux problème' (*12*, p.67), since it is clear from the
fact that Vigny used the name over a period of twenty-five years
(there are references to it in *Journal* entries for 1838), and,
indeed, from the connotations of the name itself, that 'Eva' is a
symbolic figure standing for Vigny's ideal and archetypal
woman: in the projected last line for a collection of 'Poèmes
philosophiques' on which his mind was running between 1842
and 1844, he terms her 'Femme qui n'est pas née et qui ne
mourra jamais' (*18*, p.84). We shall see that she possesses many
features in common with such female figures as Princess
Trubetskoi, and that she represents the perfect and indispensable partner for the poet, and ultimately for man in general,

[5] The most recent evidence for this contention is to be found in a double article
by P.-G. Castex (*12*, pp.12-21, 58-67).

in a relationship on which humanity's future is to be founded.

'La Maison du berger' is, however, also a poem of social and environmental pessimism. In this respect we can see it as an extension of those poems of religious, political and personal pessimism of which several were composed in the years prior to the publication of 'La Maison du berger', and which collectively constitute the 'destinée' of mankind under the old order. In 'La Maison du berger' Vigny posits the incompatability between man and his contemporary urban environment from stanza II: addressing Eva, he says:

> Si ton âme enchaînée, ainsi que l'est mon âme,
> Lasse de son boulet et de son pain amer,
> Sur sa galère en deuil laisse tomber la rame,
> Penche sa tête pâle et pleure sur la mer,
> Et, cherchant dans les flots une route inconnue,
> Y voit, en frissonnant, sur son épaule nue
> La lettre sociale écrite avec le fer (MB. 8-14)

This stanza uses Vigny's recurrent image of the 'âme enchaînée', already seen in 'Les Destinées' and 'Wanda', to represent the idea of the human spirit in an environment where it is denied the possiblity of development. It also formulates the associated concept of life as a prison, with the soul as a galley-slave (MB. 9-11), a theme which haunted Vigny, and to which a number of *Journal* entries in the 1830s are devoted. The 'route inconnue' is the road of escape, whilst the reference to the 'lettre sociale', the brand imposed on convicts sentenced to the galleys, is a grim pun: for Vigny life in the contemporary social environment is indeed comparable to a sentence in the galleys. It is the environment that he invites Eva to leave with him: 'Pars courageusement, laisse toutes les villes' (MB. 22), urban units seen as 'sombres îles' (MB. 27), amid nature's beauty.

One particular aspect of urban society is stigmatised in a section of the poem which has been much ridiculed. Vigny, like many of his fellow Romantics, feared and hated the effects of industrialisation, a process to which the wealth-creating policies of Louis-Philippe's ministers were allowing free rein. These fears were exacerbated by a visit to Birmingham in 1839 and brought to a head in the horrific Versailles railway accident of 8 May 1842 which claimed more than fifty lives, and of which Vigny wrote to Mme de la Grange: 'Quel auto-da-fé! Quel sacrifice horrible à l'Industrie!' (*4*, p.166). In the poem Vigny characterises the train as 'la vapeur foudroyante' (MB. 64) and 'le taureau de fer qui fume, souffle et beugle' (MB. 78); and he castigates those who have allowed the development of the railway for purely materialistic purposes, oblivious to the inherent dangers (MB. 78-84).

Now Vigny is certainly not opposed to progress, as 'La Bouteille à la mer' and, in a different context, 'La Sauvage', will show. He accepts that the railway can have its uses and acquiesces in its retention

> Pourvu qu'ouverts toujours aux généreuses choses,
> Les chemins du vendeur servent les passions.
>
> (MB. 94-95)

In other words he sees its potential in terms of its services to purely human values, errands of mercy to friends in distress (MB. 99-100), last visits to a dying mother (MB. 103-05), or participation in patriotic ceremonies (MB. 102). Otherwise he is less than enthusiastic — 'Evitons ces chemins' (MB. 106). Even if the railway can be made safe, its coming will destroy the pleasure of travelling, 'L'espoir d'arriver tard dans un sauvage lieu' (MB. 119), presumably by way of the 'route inconnue' (MB. 12):

> La distance et le temps sont vaincus. La science
> Trace autour de la terre un chemin triste et droit.
> Le Monde est rétréci par notre expérience
> Et l'équateur n'est plus qu'un anneau trop étroit.
> Plus de hasard. (MB. 120-24)

In other words the train represents an insidious extension of man's age-long 'destinée' under the old God and his minions, a point underlined by words such as 'rétréci' and 'anneau', which recall the idea of the imprisoning and constricting 'collier' (D. 110) of 'Les Destinées'. The railway timetable, (theoretically) accurate to the last minute, effectively removes the possibility of man exercising control over one small aspect of his own 'destinée'.

The withdrawal of the poet and Eva therefore takes place to allow them to distance themselves from urban society and the industrial menace. This withdrawal is to nature, perceived here as welcoming and kindly, offering a Lamartinian haven: 'Les grands bois et les champs sont de vastes asiles' (MB. 26). Moreover, it is made perfectly clear that this refuge in nature, the 'Maison du Berger' (MB. 49) of the title, has, as one of its purposes at least, 'l'amour et ta divine faute' (MB. 47), and that 'parmi les fleurs, nous trouverons dans l'ombre, / Pour nos cheveux unis, un lit silencieux' (MB. 55-56), the loosened 'cheveux' symbolising here, as in 'La Colère de Samson' (CS. 16), sexual activity. Thereafter the lovers' destination is uncertain — unlike the 'predestined' railway train 'Nous suivrons du hasard la course vagabonde' (MB. 61), dictated by 'la Rêverie amoureuse' (MB. 127), which will leave the poet free to meditate on his poetry.

This brings us to the vitally important second section of the poem, with its definition of the nature and purpose of poetry. Poetry, says Vigny, was originally a sacred, vatic pursuit — 'Fille du Saint Orphée'! (MB. 155) — but has become debased almost since the time of its conception (MB. 162) as a result of its use for frivolous purposes for which it was not intended. In consequence, 'les hommes les plus graves / Ne posent qu'à demi ta couronne à leur front' (MB. 169-70), a clear reference to figures such as Lamartine, for whom politics had now become the sphere of prime importance — 'n'être que poète est pour eux un affront' (MB. 172). (It is perhaps worth noting in this context that Lamartine had also made an impassioned speech in favour of the railway three days after the Versailles disaster, which can hardly have endeared him to Vigny.) In their rejection of poetry, however, they are in error, since they are preparing for them-selves the fate subsequently chronicled in 'Les Oracles': indeed Vigny may well have drawn the title for the latter poem from two lines in 'La Maison du berger' in which he describes the Chambre des Députés:

> La chambre où ces élus donnent leurs faux combats
> Jette en vain, dans son temple, un incertain *oracle*.
>
> (MB. 184-85)[6]

Again Vigny stresses the futility and invidiousness of parliamentary democracy, this time by a rather clumsy reference to the theme of industrialisation in section I of the poem. The people for whose benefit this electoral charade is supposedly played do not want it, and indeed fear it: the ordinary voter

> [...] regarde encor le jeu des assemblées
> De l'œil dont ses enfants et ses femmes troublées
> Voient le terrible essai des vapeurs aux cent bras.
>
> (MB. 187-89)

In other words, parliamentary democracy must be seen in the same light as industrialisation, another manifestation of those potentially lethal 'destinées' from which man must seek to escape. The 'avocat d'un jour' (MB. 193) who aims to make a name and a career for himself in this domain is mistaking his way: it is highly significant that the politician sees no reality in the concept of 'l'âme':

> Lui qui doute de l'âme, il croit à ses paroles.
> Poésie, il se rit de tes graves symboles.
> O toi des vrais penseurs impérissable amour!
>
> (MB. 194-96)

Hence the real purpose of poetry comes into focus. It is, we have already learned, a 'trésor', a 'perle de la pensée' (MB. 134), but feared by 'le vulgaire effrayé' (MB. 140) when seen to 'briller sur

---

[6] The link between the two poems is apparent from the first stanza, with its reference to 'la maison errante et solitaire' (O. 3), and is further underlined by a *verbatim* repetition of line 177 of 'La Maison du berger', 'Mais le sol tremble aux pieds de ces tribuns romains', in line 60 of 'Les Oracles', 'Il a croulé, *ce sol qui tremblait sous vos pieds*'. (The italics are Vigny's.)

un front mâle' (MB. 138). The reason for this is that 'Le pur enthousiasme est craint des faibles âmes' (MB. 141), and by implication only understood by and embodied in 'l'âme forte et grave' (D. 120). We recall here Vigny's observation in his *Journal* that 'le fort fait ses événements, le faible subit ceux que la destinée lui impose' (*7*, II, p.880). Poetry is therefore equated with 'enthousiasme' — 'la poésie, c'est *l'Enthousiasme cristallisé*' (*7*, II, p.1078), writes Vigny in 1837 — and the capacity of shaping one's own 'destinée'. Vigny noted in his *Journal* the importance of the correct etymological sense of 'enthousiasme': 'Ce n'est pas pour rien qu'*enthousiasme* veut dire Dieu dans nous' (*4*, p.174). Now self-evidently this God, subsequently equated with 'le Soleil du ciel ... l'Amour ... la Vie' (MB. 145), cannot be the predestinarian God of 'Les Destinées' or 'Le Mont des oliviers', but must be a new God, whose characteristics will become apparent as we, the readers, representative of humanity, progress.

The purpose of poetry, because of its divine nature, is quite simply to act as a guide for humanity towards its *new* 'destinée', and by extension the poet himself becomes, as in the works of so many Romantics, a 'mage', a guide and mentor of the new age. Poetry becomes an embodiment of all that is worthwhile in the human spirit. This is made apparent by the image of the pearl, since the precious values it enshrines will be built up by successive layers of accretion, as is the pearl inside the oyster. Vigny speaks of the pearl as destined to 'amasser les couleurs qui doivent te former' (MB. 137). He had previously used the image in *Servitude et grandeur militaires* (1835), to describe the life of Renaud, hero of 'La Canne de jonc': 'Chaque vague de la mer ajoute un voile blanchâtre aux beautés d'une perle, chaque flot travaille lentement à la rendre plus parfaite ... c'était tout à fait ainsi que s'était formé ce caractère dans de vastes bouleversements et au fond des plus sombres et perpétuelles épreuves' (*7*, II, p.664). The transference of the image is relevant: it implies that poetry is the reflection of man's character and the best values it embodies. We are thus firmly situated in an anthropocentric universe where the old, pre-existent Gods are dead, and new ones await their creation.

The image of the pearl now gives way to that of the diamond, with its multiple connotations of light, reflection, durability and, again, great price:

> Comment se garderaient les profondes pensées
> Sans rassembler leurs feux dans ton diamant pur
> Qui conserve si bien leurs splendeurs condensées?
> Ce fin miroir solide, étincelant et dur;
> Reste des nations mortes, durable pierre;
> Qu'on trouve sous ses pieds lorsque dans la poussière
> On cherche les cités sans en voir un seul mur.
>
> (MB. 197-203)

Poetry is therefore both a series of accretions and a condensation of those quintessential human values which are integral to the creation of man's new 'destinée'. It is thus, by definition, the highest form of religion: 'Les religions sont des œuvres de poésie. Elles élèvent des temples à une idée pour la faire voir de loin, et la conserver dans le trésor de la morale. Le temple vieillit, s'écroule, et laisse voir l'idée dans ses ruines, pareille à une poudre de diamant' (7, II, p.1140). Precious, durable, light-reflecting, it is also a mirror (MB. 200), in the sense that, as P.-G. Castex argues, it must be seen to reflect the poet's own vision of the world. The link provided by the 'perle' image between poetry and character helps us to understand this idea, and a *Journal* entry for 1832 introduces and further explains the image of the mirror: poetic production 'ne peut jamais être qu'un reflet des impressions reçues de la Société, mais il sera d'autant plus brillant que le miroir sera plus clarifié par la retraite et plus épuré par la flamme d'un amour extatique de la pensée et l'ardeur d'un travail opiniâtre' (7, II, p.963). This image of refinement parallels Vigny's insistence that 'l'art est la vérité choisie' (7, II, p.901). Thus the diamond of poetry, transmitted through the ages in various guises, selecting, concentrating and enshrining their wisdom, also mirrors the poet's *own* views which, subsequent to his death, will become a further accretion on the 'perle' and pass on to other poets to act as a mirror for them in turn. As we shall see, 'L'Esprit pur' will add a further twist to this already complex pattern.

The 'diamant' of poetry has, however, an immediate significance for humanity other than the poet. Its purpose is, by the light it sheds, to illuminate 'les pas lents et tardifs de l'humaine raison' (MB. 205). The poet must therefore place it on the roof of the 'Maison du Berger'. The first point to note about this intention is that it underlines the poet's solidarity with humanity, albeit at a distance. He must first *withdraw* from man in society (as seen earlier in the poem) in order validly to be able to assist him. As Vigny wrote in his *Journal* (1832): 'Quand j'ai dit: "La Solitude est sainte", je n'ai pas entendu par solitude une séparation et un oubli entier des hommes et de la Société, mais une retraite où l'âme se puisse recueillir en elle-même, puisse jouir de ses propres facultés et rassembler ses forces pour produire quelque chose de grand' (7, II, p.963). (It is perhaps rather touching that his apparently last entry in the *Journal* was a note of a heraldic device that would signify 'Saincte Solitude' (7, II, p.1392).)

The light shed by the 'diamant' will thus at one and the same time illuminate the faltering forward march of humanity and enable the poet to perceive its progress:

> Il faut, pour voir de loin les Peuples qui cheminent,
> Que le Berger t'enchâsse au toit de sa Maison.
>
> (MB. 206-07)

The second point to note is the use of the verb 'enchâsser'. This is not selected at random. Etymologically it derives from the noun 'châsse', and the unambiguous connotations are religious — poetry is the new religion of mankind. All this ties in very clearly with the novel *Daphné*, unpublished in Vigny's lifetime, in which similar ideas are advanced in similar terms to the Emperor Julian by the philosopher Libanius:

> Tu sais ce que c'est que le Trésor de Daphné: c'est l'axe du monde, c'est la sève de la terre, mon ami, c'est l'élixir de vie des hommes, distillé lentement par tous les peuples passés pour les peuples à venir: c'est la morale. (7, II, p.841)

It also renders the 'Post-scriptum' of 'Les Oracles' easier to understand. If we return to stanza VI of the 'Post-scriptum', we shall see that it is a restatement, apparently composed within eighteen months of Vigny's death, of the ideas expressed in 'La Maison du berger':

> Le DIAMANT? c'est l'art des choses idéales,
> Et ses rayons d'argent, d'or, de pourpre et d'azur
> Ne cessent de lancer les deux lueurs égales
> Des pensers les plus beaux, de l'amour le plus pur.
> Il porte du Génie et transmet les empreintes.
> Oui, de ce qui survit aux Nations éteintes
> C'est lui le plus brillant trésor et le plus dur. (O. 127-33)

It does not require more than a cursory glance to see that lines 131-33 are a reformulation of lines 201-03 of 'La Maison du berger', and that the implications of lines 127-30 link very closely with those of lines 204-07 of 'La Maison du berger'. The values enshrined in the new religion are thus essentially to be those of 'Des pensers les plus beaux, de l'amour le plus pur'. We are here concerned above all with poetry as a repository of moral values and of love for humanity (a secularised version of the commandment to 'love thy neighbour as thyself'), as exemplified, I think, in the spirit of sacrifice which is an obsessive *leitmotiv* of Vigny's work, and which we have already seen embodied in *Les Destinées* by Jesus in 'Le Mont des oliviers' and by the princess in 'Wanda'. To the allied theme of the 'cristal' (O. 112), which Vigny considers in stanza IV of the 'Post-scriptum', I shall return in the context of 'La Bouteille à la mer'.

For the moment, however, it is important to realise that Vigny is thinking in terms of future, not present, generations. In *Stello* (1832), the Docteur Noir had already made this point to the eponymous poet:

> Les œuvres immortelles sont faites pour duper la Mort en faisant survivre nos idées à notre corps ... Votre royaume n'est pas de ce monde sur lequel vos yeux sont ouverts,

mais de celui qui sera quand vos yeux seront fermés. (7, I, pp.749, 753)

Clearly there is little hope for the present, as demonstrated by the castigation visited upon it by Vigny in the sequence of poems we have already considered. The 'diamant' placed by the poet on the roof of the 'Maison du Berger' has as its purpose to reflect additional light on man's endeavours to escape from the horrors of his 'destinée'. Man *is* making gradual progress — as Vigny observed in the peroration of his reception speech at the Académie, 'l'espèce humaine est en marche pour des destinées de jour en jour meilleures et plus sereines' (7, I, p.921) — but he still has a long way to go:

Le jour n'est pas levé. — Nous en sommes encore
Au premier rayon blanc qui précède l'aurore
Et dessine la terre aux bords de l'horizon. (MB. 208-10)

Although the first hesitant steps towards universal peace and brotherhood are being taken, Vigny is too clear-sighted not to realise that

La barbarie encor tient nos pieds dans sa gaine.
Le marbre des vieux temps jusqu'aux reins nous enchaîne.
(MB. 215-16)

But despite the immobilising and enslaving 'marbre' of man's old 'destinée', Vigny is confident that 'le monde est encore à conquérir sur la Barbarie' (7, II, p.1202), and determinedly closes this section with an optimistic 'profession de foi' in the 'âme' and its attainment of that realm of moral and spiritual values where man's self-created 'destinée' lies:

L'invisible est réel. Les âmes ont leur monde
Où sont accumulés d'impalpables trésors.
Le Seigneur contient tout dans ses deux bras immenses,
Son Verbe est le séjour de nos intelligences,
Comme ici-bas l'espace est celui de nos corps.
(MB. 220-24)

We note here the persistent rejection of materialism, the emphasis on 'd'impalpables trésors'. It is these 'trésors' that, as we have seen, quite simply *are* God. But this 'Seigneur' is emphatically not the predestinarian Jehovah of 'Les Destinées', who imposed an 'immuable entrave' (D. 116) on man's highest endeavours (D. 113-14). This 'Seigneur', defined in terms which illustrate Vigny's debt to the writings of Malebranche, fosters such aspirations of the human spirit, because they represent the new 'destinée' man is creating for himself. In its simplest terms, Vigny is creating his own God to preside over his own vision of the future. Moreover the Word ('Verbe') of this God is not to be found in a previously revealed religious truth, such as the 'Loi de l'avenir' (D. 55) of 'Les Destinées', but to be discovered by the exercise of human intelligence, which Vigny described in a letter to the Crown Prince of Bavaria as 'cette Reine du monde actuel' (7, I, p.534). In a sense, Castex is surely right to remark that Vigny's God is 'le Dieu que la libre pensée du XIXe siècle veut opposer à celui de la théologie, le Dieu de la Connaissance, de la vérité rationnelle et scientifique' (4, p.174), although such a definition implies to my mind a greater dose of aridity than Vigny intended. As subsequent poems will show, although science and scientific discovery do play a large part in Vigny's ideal future, it is science always subordinated to less tangible moral and spiritual values.

The third section of 'La Maison du berger' returns to a more personal inspiration and focus. As Castex neatly formulates it, 'la Femme est ... l'indispensable auxiliaire de l'Homme dans l'élaboration de l'œuvre poétique' (4, p.189). Woman was originally conceived, so Vigny tells us, as the mitigation of the punishment of self-love devised by God 'pour punir l'Homme, sa créature, / D'avoir porté la main sur l'arbre du savoir' (MB. 227-28). This certainly causes some confusion for the reader. Is she then a creation of the old God? and if so, why? Or does she represent the first intervention of the new God, a consequence of man having already begun to seek that knowledge which is inseparable from the creation of his new 'destinée'? However this may be, she also enables man to see himself 'au miroir d'une autre âme' (MB. 234). This repetition of the term 'miroir', already used in defining poetry (MB. 200), stresses woman's role as a vital adjunct to the poet, as indeed does the reference to her 'âme', the source of poetry. Man and woman are therefore complementary in the domain of poetic creation, and the inextricability of their joint existence is stressed by the paradoxical definition of woman's function, where again Vigny's twin requirements, a woman at once maternal and submissive, are reiterated:

> C'est afin que tu sois son juge et son esclave
> Et règnes sur sa vie en vivant sous sa loi. (MB. 237-38)

Her function, which she can, like the poet, perform only in isolation, is to register the persistence of human distress:

> C'est à toi qu'il convient d'ouïr les grandes plaintes
> Que l'humanité triste exhale sourdement.
> Quand le cœur est gonflé d'indignations saintes,
> L'air des cités l'étouffe à chaque battement.
> Mais de loin les soupirs des tourmentes civiles,
> S'unissant au-dessus du charbon noir des villes,
> Ne forment qu'un grand mot qu'on entend clairement.
> (MB. 260-66)

Vigny briefly returns here to his attack on industrialisation — 'charbon noir des villes' — with which he implicitly associates human misery, characterised in an image very reminiscent of Hugo's 'Ce qu'on entend sur la montagne'. He then notes that it is woman's responsibility to 'ouïr les grandes plaintes', and to communicate the 'indignations saintes' that they inspire to the poet. The solitude of nature, however, is only a haven for Vigny when Eva is with him: indeed, more than a haven, it becomes a temple in which he can adore her as a priestess of his new religion:

> Viens donc, le ciel pour moi n'est plus qu'une *auréole*
> Qui t'entoure d'*azur*, t'éclaire et te défend;
> La montagne est ton *temple* et le bois sa *coupole*
> (MB. 267-69; my italics)

The idea of nature as a temple (the other italicised words in the quotation denote associated religious concepts) is a hackneyed Romantic *lieu commun*, dating from Chateaubriand's *Génie du christianisme*, but Vigny invests it with new connotations, for here nature becomes the environment for a secularised religion: 'la nature n'est pour moi qu'une toile de fond sur laquelle se détachent les figures humaines' (*8*, p.316). The poet, however, can only achieve this perception of the natural environment if Eva, his Muse and helpmeet, representing the human values of love and pity, is present:

> Eva, j'aimerai tout dans les choses créées,
> Je les contemplerai dans ton regard rêveur. (MB. 274-75)

The image of the mirror returns: nature must be reflected through Eva's eyes if its affective value is to be a positive one. Without Eva, nature reverts to its role as the logical extension of a hostile God and a fearsome 'destinée' (a point most clearly made in the later poem 'La Bouteille à la mer'):

> Elle me dit: 'Je suis l'impassible théâtre
> Que ne peut remuer le pied de ses acteurs;
> Mes marches d'émeraude et mes parvis d'albâtre,
> Mes colonnes de marbre ont les dieux pour sculpteurs.
> Je n'entends ni vos cris ni vos soupirs; à peine
> Je sens passer sur moi la comédie humaine
> Qui cherche en vain au ciel ses muets spectateurs.
>
> (MB. 281-87)

Nature clearly takes on here the attributes of the God of 'Les Destinées' — 'impassible' to human misery (yet it is paradoxically only in nature that the poet and Eva *can* be receptive to it) and referring once more to the silence of God: the 'muets spectateurs' of the 'comédie humaine' are clearly the representatives of the old order that man must destroy to achieve self-realisation. Moreover, Vigny tragically revalidates the Shakespearean image of the world being a stage — nature is the 'théâtre' on which the 'acteurs' play out their brief roles, and lines 283-84 similarly refer to the habitual decor of a theatre: 'marches', 'parvis', 'colonnes'. Nature's indifference and her immutable permanence render man's anguished ephemerality all the more poignant, and provoke Vigny's fierce reaction:

Et je dis à mes yeux qui lui trouvaient des charmes:
— Ailleurs tous vos regards, ailleurs toutes vos larmes,
Aimez ce que jamais on ne verra deux fois. (MB. 306-08)

It is thus that man's ephemerality becomes part of his grandeur, and his struggles take on an epic dimension. Nature is rejected in favour of humanity:

Plus que tout votre règne et que ses splendeurs vaines,
J'aime la majesté des souffrances humaines.
(MB. 320-21)

Of line 321, Vigny wrote in his *Journal* that 'ce vers est le sens de tous mes Poèmes philosophiques. L'esprit d'humanité; l'amour entier de l'humanité et de l'amélioration de ses destinées' (*7*, II, p.1219), and a note of 1835 stresses his negative view of nature: 'la nature est pour moi une décoration dont la durée est insolente, et sur laquelle est jetée cette passagère et sublime marionnette appelée l'homme' (*7*, II, p.1028). The use of the term 'majesté' suggests that the genuine majesty of human suffering in the search for a new 'destinée' displaces all the 'splendeurs vaines', not only of nature, but of the old gods and rulers of mankind, as illustrated in preceding poems. The poem closes with an invitation to Eva to transcend the ephemerality of existence — 'Nous marcherons ainsi, ne laissant que notre ombre' (MB. 330) — and the inevitable end of their love in death — for this reason Eva's love is characterised as 'taciturne et toujours menacé' (MB. 336) — by participating from the solitude of the 'Maison du Berger' in humanity's forward march:

Viens du paisible seuil de la maison roulante
Voir ceux qui sont passés et ceux qui passeront.

Tous les tableaux humains qu'un Esprit pur m'apporte
S'animeront pour toi, quand, devant notre porte,
Les grands pays muets longuement s'étendront.

(MB. 325-29)

Hence Eva, the poet's inspiration, will be enabled to see human
endeavour in two distinct ways. She will, as we have noted,
apprehend it directly in the form of the suffering against which
she urges the poet to protest. But she will also perceive it meta-
morphosed into the 'tableaux humains qu'un Esprit pur
m'apporte', a completer understanding blending real and artistic
truth, much as Vigny had advocated in the 'Réflexions sur la
vérité dans l'art'. The 'Esprit pur', the spirit of poetry and all
that Vigny's conception of poetry connotes, the new God
indeed, will return to figure prominently in 1863 in the last poem
Vigny was ever to write.

'La Maison du berger' is a long, complex and intensely
moving poem, and is central to an understanding of Vigny's
philosophy. It completes the circle of pessimism about the old
world and the values that dominate it, and begins to formulate
the values of an alternative morality to preside over man's
future. It is the first poem clearly to posit, albeit in a rather
generalised form, that new anthropocentric 'destinée' towards
which humanity must work.

5. 'La Sauvage' and 'La Flûte'

After this remarkable achievement, 'La Sauvage' and 'La Flûte' both seem rather humdrum, although they are not without significance in the elaboration of Vigny's message. 'La Sauvage', a rather maudlin tale about a Red Indian woman who finds shelter and refuge with an English colonial and his family, illustrates Vigny's view that civilisation is greatly superior to barbarism. This barbarism, or at least the environment that permits it to exist, is once again the work of the old God, for the Indians live in 'ces grands bois semés des mains de Dieu' (S. 52). But, to some degree, in this poem at least, barbarism has destroyed itself by mutual genocide, with the result that, somewhat to the Indian woman's chagrin, she is constrained to seek refuge with the settlers despised by her tribe (S. 56-58).

The importance of this poem therefore lies in the presentation of the figure of the colonial. A. Bouvet suggests that there is an element of parody in this, but frankly I doubt it. The colonial seems to me to be the model of what Vigny felt a husband and father ought to be, and the reference to his 'Papauté', (S. 106), implying his supremacy in all things, must, I fear, be accepted with a straight face: it corresponds, after all, with Vigny's firmly held view that 'l'être féminin n'aura jamais de bonheur que dans la *soumission*' (*8*, p.411). His wife, with her 'sourire angélique' (S. 123), is clearly that combination of submissive partner and 'ministering angel' for which Vigny so yearned. Most significant, however, is the fact that Vigny tells us that the colonial 'sert, / Prêtre et père a la fois, son Dieu dans un désert' (S. 107-08), and that the savage offers herself as an 'esclave' (S. 129). If we place the term 'esclave' in the frame of reference established for it by 'Les Destinées' and 'Wanda', we see that the savage, basing her interpretation of the situation on the values of the old world of barbarism (the only one she knows), offers herself to this new God (of whom the colonial is a priest) in exactly the same way as all men have been constrained to serve the God of 'Les Destinées' in the past. But the colonial is in fact only a thinly disguised version of the poet, for the God of whom he is the priest is not the old God, but the 'Seigneur' of 'La Maison du berger'. (According to the logic of the narrative, of course, he is the God of the Christians, hence strictly speaking no more than a variant on the old God of 'Les Destinées', but Vigny is not concerned with such pettifogging details as these!) The savage's offer of herself in slavery is thus refused — implicitly in line 141, 'Ma sœur ... entre dans ma famille', indicating a future relationship based on equality, and more explicitly in line 204, 'Sois donc notre convive, avec nous tu vivras'. The price she has to pay is to listen to a long harangue on the subject of where the Indians have gone wrong: they are, says the colonial,

> Sauvages animaux sans but, sans loi, sans âme,
> Pour avoir dédaigné le Travail et la femme. (S. 153-54)

By this point Vigny set great store. His prose draft for the poem includes the words, 'Ah, sauvage, tu péris dans les bois parce que tu as dédaigné la propriété et son héritage, parce que tu as méprisé le travail et que tu l'as imposé à la femme faible que tu devais adorer' (*18*, p.69). In the late twentieth century we should, I think, be greatly tempted to retort that the Indians could hardly have 'dédaigné ... la femme' much more than Vigny appears to do, but we have to accept that Vigny did not see things in quite this way. The Indians belong to the predestinarian society of the past, hence they are 'sans âme'. They have rejected civilisation, based on work (S. 145-46), and social organisation, 'la sainte union des peuples dans les villes' (S. 158), a description which, from the author of 'La Mort du loup', does admittedly have a slightly bizarre ring to it, although as I have suggested, I think the contradiction is more apparent than real.

In the context of the new society of which the colonial is the missionary, the Indians are seen as immature 'enfants' (S. 155), rejecting 'la paix, l'ordre et les lois civiles' (S. 157). In this they are in error (and ultimately they have no choice but to accept these values) for

> La Loi d'Europe est lourde, impassible et robuste,
> Mais son cercle est divin, car au centre est le Juste.
>   (S. 161-62)

'Le Juste' is a figure of increasing importance in Vigny's poetry. In the concluding 'septain' of 'Le Mont des oliviers', he is instrumental in the turning away from the old God: here he becomes instrumental in the creation of the new order. Superficially it may seem that this new order ('Loi') is little better than the one it replaces, for the Indians certainly perceive it as 'lourde'. But the answer of this 'prudente Fée' (S. 165) to such criticism is: 'Vous m'appelez la Loi, je suis la Liberté' (S. 168). This undoubtedly has implications on the political level — the fairy's proclivities lead her to found republics, not monarchies, confirming Vigny's enthusiasm for the American constitution — but its fundamental basis is to be found in what might be termed its moral implications:

> Car de la Sainte Loi tel est le caractère
> Qu'elle a de la Nature interprété les cris. (S. 182-83)

The adjective 'sainte' is, of course, not to be understood in a Christian context, but in that of the new morality, based on a concept of inheritance more fully explained in 'La Bouteille à la mer'. The colonial is working not merely for himself, but for his descendants who will continue his work (S. 179-81). Hence the poem becomes an allegory for the future of all mankind — 'nulle peuplade dorénavant n'aura le droit de rester barbare à côté des nations civilisées' (7, II, p.939) — as the savage is accepted into the civilised community and adopts its values: 'peut-être Chrétienne / Un jour ma forte Loi, femme, sera la tienne' (S. 205-06). In this broader context the concluding eulogy of motherhood takes on its fullest significance. The colonial, like the poet, is working for a future he cannot hope to see, but which his 'forte Loi' (Christianity for the narrative purposes of the poem only) is already in the process of creating.

After this rather solemn and portentous lecture, 'La Flûte' offers us a rare flash of humour as Vigny ruefully accepts that our efforts to build man's new 'destinée' are not always crowned with instant success. The flautist himself, with his ambition (F. 34-35) suggests at least in part a gentle parody of Vigny's own unrealised ambition to be a man of action. (Significantly, he had also taken flute lessons when a child.) The flautist ascribes his failure in his various endeavours to his 'pauvre âme' (F. 69), and senses that he will never succeed:

> L'idée à l'horizon est à peine entrevue,
> Que sa lumière écrase et fait ployer ma vue.
> Je vois grossir l'obstacle en invincible amas,
> Je tombe ainsi que Paul en marchant vers Damas.
> — Pourquoi, me dit la voix qu'il faut aimer et craindre,
> Pourquoi me poursuis-tu, toi qui ne peux m'étreindre?
>
> (F. 73-78)

Here the humorous treatment comes abruptly to an end, and the response to the flautist, delivered by Vigny himself (another interesting example of narrative *dédoublement* on a par with 'La Mort du loup') is on another level entirely. The flautist suffers as a result of his failure to achieve the ideal, but this suffering is to be equated less with that of the wolf in 'La Mort du loup' than with 'la majesté des souffrances humaines' (MB. 321) of 'La Maison du berger'. It is suffering with a purpose, silent like the wolf's, but explicitly positive and creative:

> Ce Sisyphe éternel est beau, seul, tout meurtri,
> Brûlé, précipité, sans jeter un seul cri,
> Et n'avouant jamais qu'il saigne et qu'il succombe
> A toujours ramasser son rocher qui retombe. (F. 95-98)

A century later, Camus wrote that 'il faut imaginer Sisyphe heureux'. That too is undoubtedly the implication of Vigny's her sententious lines: in our work for the future we contribute qually, because the 'âme' is held back, more in some than in others, by the defects of the 'corps'. Not even the most gifted amongst us can put off this Sisyphean fate (F. 103-04), and so the image of the flute finds its justification. The 'âme' of the flautist has a mental picture of the ideal sounds he wishes the instrument to produce, but the noise that actually issues forth is not quite of the same calibre. This, however, is not his fault:

> Eh bien, c'est au bois lourd que sont tous les défauts,
> Votre souffle était juste et votre chant est faux.
>
> (F. 119-20)

In this world, therefore, we must accept that we have limitations, but nonetheless work to our fullest capacity within them in order to assist in the creation of man's new 'destinée'. Here, for the first time, Vigny offers encouragement not just to the 'fort', but also to the 'faible courageux' (F. 91). At least, so it seems, there is the consolation of achieving equality in the afterlife, unencumbered by our variously inadequate physical envelopes, in the presence of the 'Seigneur' of 'La Maison du berger':

> Je crois qu'après la mort, quand l'union s'achève,
> L'âme retrouve alors la vue et la clarté...
> Et, calme, elle reprend, dans l'idéal bonheur,
> La sainte égalité des esprits du Seigneur.
>
> (F. 122-23, 131-32)

It seems probable that Vigny thought quite highly of this poem, since he noted a summary of its meaning in his *Journal* (*7*, II, p.1303) and contemplated a further elaboration of the theme in the form of a novel (*7*, II, p.1365). But it is difficult to avoid the impression that, despite some poetry of high quality, Vigny would have been better advised to stick to the Sisyphus image and eschew the somewhat saccharin glibness of 'La sainte égalité des esprits du Seigneur', to which I am unsure whether he would in reality have paid more than lip-service. A more convincing concept of immortality, faith in a terrestrial, rather then celestial, afterlife, is contained in 'La Bouteille à la mer'.

6. 'La Bouteille à la mer', 'L'Esprit pur', the Epigraph

'La Bouteille à la mer' can be seen as an expansion and refinement of the more generalised message contained in 'La Maison du berger'. Its focus is primarily on the 'fonction du poète', embodied in the form of an allegorical sea-story, and its subtitle is 'Conseil à un jeune homme inconnu'. Here there is, I think, an intentional pun, for 'inconnu' can mean either 'unknown' in the sense of 'not yet famous', or 'unknown' in the sense that Vigny has no idea whom he is addressing. In the former sense, Vigny is offering encouragement in terms of the young poet's future literary endeavours: in the latter, perhaps ultimately more significantly, he is transmitting a lesson to each and every one of us, his readers, about his vision of the world and the future.[7] However this may be, the opening stanza of the poem is extremely important:

> Courage, ô faible enfant, de qui ma solitude
> Reçoit ces chants plaintifs, sans nom, que vous jetez
> Sous mes yeux ombragés du camail de l'étude.
> Oubliez les enfants par la mort arrêtés;
> Oubliez Chatterton, Gilbert et Malfilâtre;
> De l'œuvre d'avenir saintement idolâtre,
> Enfin, oubliez l'homme en vous-même. — Ecoutez:
>
> (BM. 1-7)

The 'jeune homme' is, like the flautist in 'La Flûte', 'faible' (F. 70), feeling himself liable to succumb to the inexorable pressure of his 'destinée' as so many of his predecessors have done. By his triple use of the imperative 'oubliez' (BM. 4, 5, 7) Vigny urges

[7] M. Tournier refers the point about the real existence of the 'jeune poète ïconnu' to a letter written by Vigny about 1860: 'J'ai reçu un jour une ode gnifique d'un poète inconnu. J'y ai répondu par un poème qu'on trouvera s mon prochain volume' (6, p.126). The odd thing here is that Vigny had ady published the poem in 1854: so why does he not mention it by name?

him not to do so, but to maintain his Sisyphean endeavours. He must forget the three poets mentioned in line 5, all of whom, in Shakespearean phrase, despaired and died, a counsel more significant than it might appear, since Vigny in his novel *Stello* (1832) had commemorated the fates of Gilbert and Chatterton, and had gone on to base a play on the latter. Now he impresses upon his new 'unknown' disciple the need to turn from present contemplation of their failure to devote himself to the future — he must be 'De l'œuvre d'avenir saintement idolâtre'. Once again we must see this sanctity as pertaining to the new God of 'La Maison du berger', and the use of the adjective 'idolâtre' again underlines the status of poetry as a new religion. The new element in the equation, however, is the theme of self-forgetfulness, which will become a vital component of the symbolism of the poem.

It is probably not helpful to analyse the allegory of the narrative too closely (as critics have noted, there are a number of inconsistencies), but Vigny's intention is clearly to equate the captain of the ship with the poet. This worker for the future is aware that at certain moments in life man's old 'destinée' will strike back with lethal consequences:

— A de certains moments, l'âme est sans résistance;
Mais le penseur s'isole et n'attend d'assistance
Que de la forte foi dont il est embrasé. (BM. 19-21)

The use of the keyword 'âme' immediately situates the poet-captain amongst the proponents of Vigny's new religion, a point stressed by the reference to his 'forte foi', with the verb 'embrasé' echoing the eulogy of enthusiasm in 'La Maison du berger' — 'La vie est double dans les flammes' (MB. 143). The need for solitude, a principal theme of 'La Maison du berger', is also restated in line 20 — it is pointless for the poet-captain to collude with the values of the old world (as demonstrated in 'La Mort du loup') — they must be disdained (as by 'le Juste' in 'Le Mont des oliviers') even though they will ultimately destroy him:

Il voit les masses d'eau, les toise et les mesure,
Les méprise en sachant qu'il en est écrasé. (BM. 15-16)

The waters of the ocean are an emissary, cold, cruel, and impersonal (like nature in 'La Maison du berger') of the old God. They destroy indiscriminately everything in their path. But in 'La Bouteille à la mer' the victim evaluates the waves that will annihilate him, and scorns their destructive force: a secularised version of Pascal's 'roseau pensant', man can rise superior to his own fate.

> — Il se résigne, il prie; il se recueille, il pense
> A Celui qui soutient les pôles et balance
> L'équateur hérissé des longs méridiens. (BM. 26-28)

This is certainly stoic resignation, but, as we shall see, resignation with a purpose, the subject of the poet-captain's meditations being 'Celui qui soutient les pôles', the new God of 'La Maison du berger'. Such resignation contrasts sharply with the attitude of Jesus in 'Le Mont des oliviers' (and it is certainly worth noting that 'La Bouteille à la mer' immediately follows 'Le Mont des oliviers' in the ordering of this collection): whereas Jesus 'renonce' (MO. 133), i.e., gives up, the poet-captain accepts his fate, but does not for all that give up what he has already achieved, as Jesus had seemed to do:

> Son sacrifice est fait; mais il faut que la terre
> Recueille du travail le pieux monument.
> C'est le journal savant, le calcul solitaire,
> Plus rare que la perle et que le diamant;
> C'est la carte des flots faite dans la tempête,
> La carte de l'écueil qui va briser sa tête:
> Aux voyageurs futurs sublime testament. (BM. 29-35)

This stanza is, I think, central to the meaning of the poem. It underlines the role of the poet-captain — he is a Christ-figure, who has sacrificed himself, but with a purpose (a new departure in Vigny, where as we have seen, sacrifice is usually an end in itself, producing no tangible results). Once again religious imagery is employed to describe his achievement — it is a 'pieux monument' because of its role in the establishment of the new

religion of poetry. This 'pieux monument' has been elaborated
in solitude — it is a 'calcul solitaire', more precious than jewels,
a point made again slightly more elaborately in line 153. (I think
that the words 'perle' and 'diamant' are here to be understood as
having a literal significance, since in Vigny's symbolic language
the 'pieux monument' is already a 'perle' and a 'diamant'.) It is
knowledge, and a particular type of knowledge, which increases
man's awareness of the world in which he is condemned to live,
a world which has destroyed the poet-captain, but of which this
particular feature, the 'écueil', will never again destroy a human
being, because he has mapped it for the 'voyageurs futurs'. In
other words, he has conquered forever this particular aspect of
man's previous 'destinée' whilst undergoing it himself.

The series of 'flashbacks' induced by the poet-captain's
entrusting of the log-book to the bottle induces Vigny to insert a
stanza (no. XII) which has puzzled some critics. It is worth
quoting in full:

> O superstition des amours ineffables,
> Murmures de nos cœurs qui nous semblez des voix,
> Calculs de la science, ô décevantes fables!
> Pourquoi nous apparaître en un jour tant de fois?
> Pourquoi vers l'horizon nous tendre ainsi des pièges?
> Espérances roulant comme roulent les neiges;
> Globes toujours pétris et fondus sous nos doigts!
>
> (BM. 78-84)

P.-G. Castex asks: 'La "superstition des amours ineffables"
désigne-t-elle les erreurs nées dans l'imagination de ceux qui sont
restés ou bien celle des marins?' (*4*, p.227). Somewhat hesitantly
he opts for the former, referring it to the sailor's daughter who
'cherche à ramener l'aimant avec le fer' (BM. 74): 'ainsi apparaît
mieux la continuité avec la strophe précédente' (*4*, p.227). This is
rather implausible, if only because the preceding stanza ends
with the image of the sailor's wife, who, waving to her husband
leaving on board the doomed ship, 'ne sent pas ses pieds
enfoncés dans la mer' (BM. 77). It seems more likely that the
stanza represents an ambiguity deliberately introduced by

Vigny: in the face of the devotion characterised in stanzas X and
XI, it is surely natural to wonder whether work such as that
undertaken by the poet-captain and his crew, involving danger
and ultimately death, is really worth the effort, that the effort is
not just wasted on 'décevantes fables'. Certainly line 79 seems to
bear some resemblance to the famous 'voix qu'il faut aimer et
craindre' (F. 77), and the rhetorical questions of line 85, 'Où
sont-ils à présent? Où sont ces trois cents braves?' would seem
further to confirm this interpretation: *have* their lives been
wasted? Perhaps Vigny is too honest not to allow at least a
suspicion of this to cross his reader's minds, but the rest of the
poem will refute this hesitation.

As the ship sinks, the poet-captain throws the bottle into the
sea 'et salue / Les jours de l'avenir qui pour lui sont venus' (BM.
97-98). This may refer to his impending departure towards the
Heaven evoked in 'La Flûte' — the 'sainte égalité des esprits du
Seigneur' (F. 132) — but more probably it points forward to the
next stanza:

> Il sourit en songeant que ce fragile verre
> Portera sa pensée et son nom jusqu'au port;
> Que d'une île inconnue il agrandit la terre;
> Qu'il marque un nouvel astre et le confie au sort;
> Que Dieu peut bien permettre à des eaux insensées
> De perdre des vaisseaux, mais non pas des pensées,
> Et qu'avec un flacon il a vaincu la mort. (BM. 99-105)

Here, far more than in the rather vapid Heaven of 'La Flûte', is
Vigny's real notion of what constitutes life after death. The
poet-captain's 'forte foi' in the new God means that, unlike
Jesus in 'Le Mont des oliviers', he bequeathes to posterity a
positive achievement for which he will be remembered: he
conquers death by virtue of his role as one of the creators of
man's new 'destinée'. Whereas the old God was determined to
stifle human endeavour, the new one is just as determined to
foster it.

The bottle containing the poet-captain's life's work is thus
cast into the sea: the medium that destroyed the creator will

contribute to the salvation of his creation. In its function, the bottle is similar to the central image of *Daphné*, the 'momie', preserved by a transparent 'cristal':

> Les dogmes religieux ... sont pareils à ce cristal. Ils con-
> servent le peu de sages préceptes que les races se sont
> formés et se passent l'une à l'autre. Lorsque l'un de ces
> cristaux sacrés s'est brisé sous l'effort des siècles..., alors le
> trésor public est en danger, et il faut qu'un nouveau cristal
> serve à le voiler de ses emblèmes. (7, II, p.843)

In the past, religious dogma, 'le cristal', guarded the eternal verities, 'le trésor'. In 'La Sauvage', Vigny had used the image in a more literal sense, where 'Un billet en dix mots qu'écrivit Washington' (S. 116) is protected 'sous un cristal pur' (S. 115). In the same way, the bottle guards the poet-captain's log-book, a new 'cristal' preserving a new 'trésor'. But Vigny's prose draft for the poem stressed that the bottle was 'sacrée', and thereafter made it clear (a point repeated in the *Journal*, but not actually taken over into the poem) that 'la bouteille qui porte ta pensée se nomme Imprimerie' (*18*, pp.76-77). In other words, poetry in the form of the printed word will now carry the 'trésor' to future generations. What is more, the 'cristal', once identified with 'Imprimerie', can cease to be the purely passive vessel containing the 'momie', and can take on an active role: hence we find the transformation of the concept of the 'cristal' in the 'Post-scriptum' of 'Les Oracles':

> Le cristal, c'est la Vue et la Clarté du JUSTE,
> Du principe éternel de toute vérité,
> L'examen de soi-même au tribunal auguste
> Où la Raison, l'Honneur, la Bonté, l'Equité,
> La Prévoyance à l'œil rapide et la Science
> Délibèrent en paix devant la Conscience
> Qui, jugeant l'action, régit la Liberté. (O. 113-19)

Now I would be the last to claim that Vigny's definition of 'le cristal' is, so to speak, crystal-clear: there are far too many abstract nouns and capital letters for that. I find A. Bouvet's attempt to decipher Vigny's meaning helpfully lucid here: 'Le *cristal* c'est ce qu'ailleurs Vigny appelle l' "atticisme", le regard limpide que le poète dirige sur les "choses idéales", sur lui-même et sur le monde' (5, p.70). This is confirmed by the description of 'le cristal' as a 'rempart des grandes âmes' (O. 120). He goes on to relate the 'cristal' to the 'microscope' (O. 104), thereby stressing the way in which it can become a means of analysing and dissecting the modern world (as indeed 'Les Oracles' and 'Wanda' both prove). It is worth noting, moreover, that the image of the 'microscope' once again *distances* the poet from the world — 'Saincte Solitude' yet again.

It is something of a relief to turn once again to the bottle and its journey. The religious connotations of this journey are stressed by line 112, 'Mais elle vient de l'arche et porte le rameau'. This implied equation of the bottle with the dove from Noah's Ark will take on its full significance only in the context of 'L'Esprit pur', but the image clearly suggests a new beginning, like that of mankind after the Flood. We might note in passing that Vigny deliberately falsifies the Biblical story, in which the dove *returns* to the Ark bearing the olive branch. It is probably not altogether fanciful to suggest that Vigny is here reasserting the peace-bringing potential of poetry, first adumbrated in 'La Maison du berger' (MB. 211-17). The bottle's 'destinées' (BM. 117) seem at first to be on a par with the physical fate of its creator, but a symbolic change of season 'changeant ses destinées' (BM.117) enables it to progress towards the Equator. This change is allied with the curious episode recounted in stanzas XVIII and XIX. A 'navire' (BM. 123) puts out a boat to pick up 'la Bouteille aux gens de mer sacrée' (BM. 124): however, it seems that the sound of combat nearby between 'Corsaires' (BM. 127) and a 'Négrier' (BM. 128) causes the 'navire', now referred to as a 'Frégate' (BM. 131) to recall its boat and set off again under full steam and sail. I think the meaning of this little episode is plain: the failure of the 'Frégate' to pick up the bottle because of the vicinity of the 'Négrier' symbolises humanity's failure to act upon the ideas of its great men because of unfavourable circumstances. Slavery

and piracy are as retrogressive in terms of man's development as
is the presence of their representatives in the poem in impeding
the rescue of the bottle. A longer period of time is needed before
these ideas can achieve the status they merit.

The casting-up of the bottle on the coast of France unleashes
both from Vigny and (rather improbably) from those who find it
a paean of praise. The content of the bottle is 'l'élixir divin que
boivent les esprits, / Trésor de la pensée et de l'expérience' (BM.
149-50). Once again religious imagery is used ('l'élixir divin'),
together with the noun 'trésor', which equates the content of the
bottle with the 'trésor! perle de la pensée' (MB. 134) which is
poetry. (Both terms also link back to *Daphné*.) The poet-captain
is now honoured, posthumously, for his discovery (BM. 159-61),
and, in the concluding three stanzas, Vigny broadens the scope
of his poem to provide a key to his entire poetic philosophy.
Here at last we have a fuller definition of what it is that Vigny
perceives as the fruitful fields for human endeavour in the
creation of man's new 'destinée':

Souvenir éternel! gloire à la découverte
Dans l'homme ou la nature égaux en profondeur,
Dans le Juste et le Bien, source à peine entr'ouverte,
Dans l'Art inépuisable, abîme de splendeur!

(BM. 162-65)

Endeavour in these fields achieves immortality, the only
immortality that really counts being the 'souvenir éternel' of
future generations. We recall the Docteur Noir's adjuration to
Stello (quoted above, pp.50-51), in which it is hardly necessary
to point out yet another Christ-parallel in the words 'Votre
royaume n'est pas de ce monde'. But it should also be noted that
the lines quoted above stress the fact that 'La Bouteille à la mer'
is not in the last analysis a poem about scientific discovery,
which explains my persistent references to the *poet*-captain.
Certainly the discoveries may be about the natural world, and
indeed, on one level, in 'La Bouteille à la mer' we are concerned
with the revelation of 'une île inconnue' (BM. 101). But the
poem, as I have already stated, is really an *allegory* of the

process of human endeavour, and therefore should not be taken literally. Significantly, although Vigny terms discoveries in the human and natural realms as 'égaux en profondeur', all his examples are taken from the former, both aesthetic and moral. This point applies even more evidently to the qualities celebrated in stanza IV of the 'Post-scriptum' of 'Les Oracles' (quoted above, p.67). Primarily, therefore, I would argue that Vigny's 'brave new world' is to be envisaged in moral and spiritual terms — he himself defined his purpose in 1835 as 'moraliser la nation et la spiritualiser' (7, II, p.1031) — the discoveries to be made by those pioneers who can collectively be grouped together under the title of 'le Juste'.

'La Bouteille à la mer' concludes with a eulogy of those pioneers. Their achievement is unlikely to be recognised in their lifetime — 'Sur la pierre des morts croît l'arbre de grandeur' (BM. 168) — but the reward for all those working, as it were, at the coal-face is the prospect of recognition by future generations. Thus Paradise is constituted by posthumous applause for our efforts on behalf of those who follow us (BM. 169-70). We can, all of us, disdain any obstacles the old world may set against us, secure in the knowledge that what we achieve in the field of human endeavour will be passed on to succeeding generations: 'L'or pur doit surnager, et sa gloire est certaine' (BM. 173), a very unscientific image which nonetheless recalls, in order to negate, the assertion of God in 'Les Destinées': 'L'Homme sera toujours un nageur incertain' (D. 83). The new God, the God of the poet-captain's 'forte foi' (BM. 21), will not permit this achievement to be lost:

> Le vrai Dieu, le Dieu fort est le Dieu des idées!
> Sur nos fronts où le germe est jeté par le sort,
> Répandons le savoir en fécondes ondées;
> Puis, recueillant le fruit tel que de l'âme il sort,
> Tout empreint du parfum des saintes solitudes,
> Jetons l'œuvre à la mer, la mer des multitudes:
> — Dieu la prendra du doigt pour la conduire au port.
>
> (BM. 176-82)

This final stanza is again heavily loaded with Vigny's keywords. We note, for example, the presence once again of the term 'âme', the source of all positive values in Vigny; we note, too, the reprise of the theme of 'La Flûte', that we may all be unequally gifted by life: it is 'le sort' that decides where 'le germe' is sown. Finally we observe once more the insistence on the need for solitude — 'Seul et libre, accomplir sa mission' (7, I, p.752) — a theme we have already seen treated in great detail in 'La Maison du berger'. Need to Solitude .

The great virtue of 'La Bouteille à la mer', therefore, at least in the context of the elaboration of Vigny's doctrine, is to elucidate the *nature* of the new religion and that of the God who presides over it, and to stress the importance of the future as the dimension in which Vigny is operating. The doctrinal edifice is now virtually complete. The function of 'L'Esprit pur' is to move from the general to the particular, and to allow Vigny, in his last poem, to situate himself as an individual in relation to the creed he has elaborated.

V.-L. Saulnier has called 'L'Esprit pur' 'peut-être le plus beau poème de notre langue' (*3*, p.IX), which is perhaps rather an exaggeration, although it is a fine and moving testament to a man within six months of death from stomach cancer. It is dedicated to Eva, although, as Castex notes, this is hardly very significant in the event, since she disappears from the poem after line 2, and Vigny himself takes the centre of the stage. Those two lines do, however, characterise Vigny's final disavowal of the importance of the privileges of birth:

Si l'Orgueil prend ton cœur quand le Peuple me nomme,
Que de mes livres seuls te vienne ta fierté. (EP. 1-2)

The only aristocracy to which he wishes to belong is the aristocracy of the intelligence: as early as 1829 he had noted in his *Journal* that his aim was to 'soumettre le monde à la domination sans bornes des esprits supérieurs en qui réside la plus grande partie de l'intelligence divine' (*7*, II, p.897). Ultimately it is only he (paradoxically deprived of descendants) who has added lustre to the name of Vigny, not through those traditional aristocratic pursuits enumerated in stanzas III-VI, and practised by his forbears, but through the medium of literature:

> — A peine une étincelle a relui dans leur cendre.
> C'est en vain que d'eux tous le sang m'a fait descendre;
> Si j'écris leur histoire, ils descendront de moi.
>
> (EP. 12-14)

In this context he himself becomes that 'reste des nations mortes' (MB. 201) of which he wrote in 'La Maison du berger'. The testimony to his own life will be very different from that accorded to his ancestors, confirming the prescription of 'La Bouteille à la mer', in which honour is due 'Aux héros du savoir plus qu'à ceux des batailles' (BM. 159), to the man who can teach posterity 'Comme son temps vivait et comment il sut vivre' (EP. 41):

> [...] Ici passaient deux races de la Gaule
> Dont le dernier vivant monte au temple et s'inscrit,
> Non sur l'obscur amas des vieux noms inutiles,
> Des Orgueilleux méchants et des Riches futiles,
> Mais sur le pur tableau des titres de L'ESPRIT.
>
> (EP. 45-49)

Once again the secularised religious imagery is very much to the fore. The 'temple' is that of the 'Dieu des idées' (BM. 176), or, in the terms of this poem, that of 'L'ESPRIT'. The title of the poem had been foreshadowed by Vigny in 'La Maison du berger' by a reference to 'Tous les tableaux humains qu'un Esprit pur m'apporte' (MB. 327), hence we can interpret this 'Esprit pur' to mean a synthesis of all those values — 'Trésor de la pensée et de l'expérience' (BM. 150) — that Vigny holds dear, combined with the inspiration or 'enthousiasme' that transmutes them into poetry. And now, having reached the 'temple', Vigny intones an anthem of praise to the new God:

> Ton règne est arrivé, PUR ESPRIT, Roi du Monde!

Quand ton aile d'Azur dans la nuit nous surprit,
Déesse de nos mœurs, la Guerre vagabonde
Régnait sur nos aïeux. — Aujourd'hui, c'est l'ECRIT.

                                                      (EP. 50-53)

Here Vigny harks back again to 'La Maison du berger' and the awakening of the concept of universal brotherhood, epitomised by the cessation of conflict between warring races (MB. 213-14), and where the 'aile d'Azur' is represented by the 'premier rayon blanc qui précède l'aurore' (MB. 209). That internecine strife between man and man which, like all human activity, takes place 'en présence de Dieu' (CS. 36) — we notice that war is referred to as a 'déesse' — now gives way to the reign of the 'Esprit' and the values enshrined in those symbols — 'perle', 'diamant', 'cristal', — variously used to characterise it. In a reference to the previous evocation of the bottle — 'Mais elle vient de l'arche et porte le rameau' (BM. 112) — he now describes 'L'ECRIT UNIVERSEL' (EP. 54) as a 'Colombe au bec d'airain! VISIBLE SAINT-ESPRIT!' (EP. 56). The 'Esprits' (D. 102) who were the 'destinées' have given way to the new Holy Ghost. No clearer substitution of the old theocentric religion by the new secular one could be made.

This, then, is Vigny's testament. It is pointless and pettifogging to jib at it by pointing out that events at the time of its writing certainly did not suggest that universal peace was about to break out, or that man was (and continues to be) a wolf to man in spite of Vigny's hailing of the coming of the kingdom of the 'PUR ESPRIT', the kingdom on earth of the true God. This stanza is the product of 'enthousiasme', an inspired vision of an inevitable event. Since, at the time of writing the poem, Vigny must at least have suspected himself to be mortally ill, we cannot but admire his courage.

The last two stanzas represent the coda of the symphony of which 'L'Esprit pur' is the final movement. Vigny qualifies himself as one who has endeavoured to sustain 'L'IDEAL du Poète et des graves Penseurs' (EP. 60). Despite his literary silence, he is convinced of the durability of his art:

J'éprouve sa durée en vingt ans de silence,
Et toujours, d'âge en âge encor, je vois la France
Contempler mes tableaux et leur jeter des fleurs.

(EP. 61-63)

The prophetic vein signifies that, like the poet-captain of 'La Bouteille à la mer', he knows that he is working for a future that appreciates him and will immortalise him:

Jeune Postérité d'un vivant qui vous aime!
Mes traits dans vos regards ne sont pas effacés;
Je peux, en ce miroir, *me connaître moi-même*;
Juges toujours nouveaux de nos travaux passés!
Flots d'amis renaissants! — Puissent mes Destinées
Vous amener à moi, de dix en dix années
Attentifs à mon œuvre, et pour moi c'est assez!

(EP. 64-70)

The eyes of posterity, Vigny's true descendants, are a mirror for his poetic achievement, just as poetry itself is a mirror of essential values — 'Ce fin miroir solide, étincelant et dur' (MB. 200), and Vigny is validated in his endeavours by this mirror, just as previously he was sustained by mirroring himself in Eva's eyes (MB. 234).[8] As if to make his point doubly clear, in line 68, Vigny introduces the word 'Destinées', to underline the fact that in this, his last poem, he has finally created his own 'destinée', casting off forever the shackles of the old world and its values that he so greatly despised.

I wrote of 'L'Esprit pur' as the coda to the symphony of *Les Destinées*. In a sense this is true. Yet I tend to agree with Castex's view that the two stanzas collected in the Gallimard edition as 'L'Age d'or de l'avenir' ('Réponse d'Eva') should be integrated into the collection. The lines, I feel, are self-explanatory in their testimony to the ultimate triumph of the human spirit:

---

[8] Vigny's discarded titles for this poem, 'Le Musée idéal' and 'L'Epreuve du temps', both underline this point.

Le rideau s'est levé devant mes yeux débiles,
La lumière s'est faite et j'ai vu ses splendeurs;
J'ai compris nos destins par ces ombres mobiles
Qui se peignaient en noir sur de vives couleurs.
Ces feux, de ta pensée étaient les lueurs pures,
Ces ombres, du passé les magiques figures,
J'ai tressailli de joie en voyant nos grandeurs.

Il est donc vrai que l'homme est monté par lui-même
Jusqu'aux sommets glacés de sa vaste raison,
Qu'il y peut vivre en paix sans plainte et sans blasphème,
Et mesurer le monde et sonder l'horizon.
Il sait que l'univers l'écrase et le dévore;
Plus grand que l'univers qu'il juge et qui l'ignore,
Le Berger a lui-même éclairé sa maison. (AOA. 1-14)

*   *   *   *   *

It is only now, as we reach the end of this survey of the poems of *Les Destinées*, that the epigraph 'C'était écrit!', which Vigny had included in his plan of 1856, takes on its full significance. The 'Colombe au bec d'airain' (EP. 56) is a rather awkwardly condensed image for the transmission of Vigny's new secular religion by the act of writing. For the 'bec d'airain' stands for the nib of the pen, a transformation of the 'doigt d'airain' and 'pieds d'airain' (D. 11, 37) of the 'destinées', and produces the 'New Testament', 'L'ECRIT UNIVERSEL, parfois impérissable' (EP. 54). The germ of the future is thus contained in the dove's 'writings': this dove is now at one and the same time the secular equivalent of the one sent forth from Noah's Ark (as we have already seen in our discussion of 'La Bouteille à la mer') and of the dove in whose shape the Holy Ghost descended on Christ after his baptism. In this way the grim parody of this event enacted in the return of the goddesses to earth in 'Les Destinées' (D. 79-96) is neutralised and expunged; in this way, too, the real crime of the Czar in 'Wanda' takes on its fullest and most blasphemous significance. But the most profound meaning of the epigraph is as a reply to the question posed in the last lines of

'Les Destinées': 'Notre mot éternel est-il: C'ETAIT ECRIT?' (D. 121). This cryptic query really means: must the predestination of the old order last for ever?

    — SUR LE LIVRE DE DIEU, dit l'Orient esclave;
Et l'Occident répond: — SUR LE LIVRE DU CHRIST.

                             (D. 122-23)

In terms of revealed religion, the answer to the question is doubly 'yes'. But the whole purpose of *Les Destinées*, the quintessential meaning of the title, is to show that the old 'destinée' *can* be replaced by a new one, that the idea of predestination enshrined in the phrase 'C'était écrit' can yield to a new human liberty of which the essence is to be found in values embodied in poetry. In this respect writing takes on a new liberating role (hence the epigraph is in fact a pun), in direct contradiction to the old constricting one, predestination tangibly contained in the written texts of the revealed religions that weighed man down. It is surely in this respect above all that 'Le Berger a lui-même éclairé sa maison' (AOA. 14).

7. *The Symbols and Image-Patterns of* Les Destinées

One of the most striking aspects of this collection of apparently disparate poems, composed over a period of twenty-five years, is the remarkable consistency of the imagery employed by Vigny to convey his ideas and message. As we have already seen, it is impossible to speak of the meaning of this poetry without constant reference to some of these images, specifically the closely interrelated ones of 'trésor', 'cristal', 'perle' and 'diamant', for they embody within themselves Vigny's entire concept of the new human 'destinée', to which he aspires: the poet here creates his own myth of the future. Set against this recurrent imagery, however, we find a wide range of image-patterns which characterise the old world, and the related concept of metaphysical 'destinée'. To these patterns I now wish to turn, to show how they reinforce the meaning and message of *Les Destinées*, and how their recurrence contributes to the unity of the overall design.

Central to Vigny's symbolic presentation of the old world are two persistent images, that of the desert and that of physical weight. Connected with the latter is that of the experience of oppression (its moral equivalent), inflicted either by mankind or by the elements. In addition, we frequently find the use of nocturnal imagery, with what might be seen as its metaphorical corollary, mourning, and a tendency to employ references to fire in a similar context. Not all these images appear in all the poems, although some (notably that of the desert) are very prevalent: but all are employed with sufficient regularity to make it apparent that for the author they represent a form of code or key to the meaning of poetry.

The desert may be seen as the archetypal image of human misery in *Les Destinées*, perhaps by virtue of its implicit contrast with the verdant pastures of Paradise, out from which God cast Adam and Eve: in the words of Adam in Milton's *Paradise Lost*,

The most extended use of the image of the desert, however, seems to me to be made in 'La Sauvage', a poem which reposes precisely on the contrast between old and new worlds. Here a poem well-known to Vigny, 'all places else / Inhospitable appear, and desolate' (XI, 305-06). Vigny certainly does not believe literally in the existence of the Garden of Eden: indeed, he is at pains to insist from the first lines of the first poem of the collection, 'Les Destinées', with its reference to 'le premier jour de la création' (D. 1), that he rejects the doctrine of the Fall. It is, however, a convenient myth: in Vigny's poetry the desert becomes the embodiment of all those aspects of the human condition which detract from or directly oppose the movement towards the desired anthropocentric 'destinée', the 'terre promise' (BM. 169) or Paradise which, for Vigny, exists only in the future. In 'Les Oracles', therefore, it is enshrined in the concept of democratic government as practised by the Orleans monarchy — 'Toute Démocratie est un désert de sables' (O. 66) — and in the legal basis on which that regime rather unsteadily reposes: 'le sable mouvant des Constitutions' (O. 25). In 'Les Destinées', it represents the endless, prospectless, purposeless existence of all men under the dominion of the old God — 'Tous errant, sans étoile, en un désert sans fond' (D. 9) — whilst in 'La Colère de Samson' and 'Le Mont des oliviers' it takes on a more personal and individual (though persistently metaphysical) significance in the context of the hostile environment in which Samson and Jesus have to wage their respective battles: for Samson, it is comfortlessly 'muet' (CS. 1), for Jesus a lonely place, as much moral and metaphorical as physical, surrounded and cut off from help by the 'nuage en deuil' (MO. 24). Wanda's sister is one of the many who 's'en vont au désert' (W. 128) of the Czar's autocracy, whilst the wolf perishes in the arid landscape of 'la bruyère épaisse' and 'les hautes brandes' (ML. 5). Others are more fortunate, since they contrive to escape: Eva flees with the poet from the urban desert to woods and fields which offer 'de vastes asiles, / Libres comme la mer autour des sombres îles' (MB, 26-27). The flautist is rescued from the 'flots noirs et déserts' (F. 60), and the bottle in the 'mouvant désert' (BM. 135) of the ocean is similarly fortunate.

The most extended use of the image of the desert, however, seems to me to be made in 'La Sauvage', a poem which reposes precisely on the contrast between old and new worlds. Here

Vigny indulges in a rather *recherché* pun, for in the first line he characterises the geographical 'Nouveau Monde' for what it actually is — a desert, embodying the values of the past, violence and barbarism. 'Solitudes que Dieu fit pour le Nouveau Monde' (S. 1) — it is indeed a world after the old God's own heart (if he has one). Not for nothing is the etymology of 'solitudes' the Latin 'solitudo', a desert. In this desert, the pioneer has established the law of European civilisation, the new law which must ultimately lead to the creation of a new 'destinée': 'sans autel, il sert, / Prêtre et père à la fois, son Dieu dans un désert' (S. 107-08). The poem brings us full circle to the myth of the lost paradise and its consequences. The 'sauvage' herself represents the tribe of Abel, who 'va dans ses forêts vides / Voir errer et mourir ses familles livides' (S. 149-50), whereas the pioneer, in his own words, represents the tribe of Cain: 'Caïn le laboureur a sa revanche ici' (S. 148). This is, on the surface, a distinctly odd remark for an apparently God-fearing man to make (the book of Genesis relates that 'the Lord had respect unto Abel and to his offering: but unto Cain and his offering he had not respect' (4, 4)), until we realise that the God whom the pioneer serves is really Vigny's new God, in the context of which his espousal of the cause of Cain makes sense. Cain and his family (amongst whom Vigny self-evidently numbers himself) are thus given a positive role: not merely do they despise and reject the old God, but in that desert created by him they build civilisation, the real New World, Paradise, an intellectual rather than a geographical concept.

Sheer crushing physical weight also seems to be an integral part of the forces of reaction in Vigny's poetic universe: with it, hand in hand, and sometimes indistinguishable from it, goes the concept of moral oppression, symbolised by the image of slavery. This imagery fittingly dominates the opening poem of the collection, 'Les Destinées': the notion of apparently physical weight is the first concept introduced in the poem (D. 2-3). Clearly, however, this is a metaphor for the mental enslavement of man by the regime of the old God and his instruments, the 'destinées', omnipresent and omnipotent, who keep mankind yoked like beasts of burden in the desert of human existence:

Ces froides déités liaient le joug de plomb
Sur le crâne et les yeux des Hommes leurs esclaves,
Tous errant, sans étoile, en un désert sans fond. (D. 7-9)

In 'La Maison du berger' it is more specifically the social than
the metaphysical dimension which is characterised by images of
weight, an environment from which the poet and Eva seek to
flee: again, the poem opens on just such an image, character-
ising both physical and moral oppression:

Si ton cœur, gémissant du poids de notre vie,
Se traîne et se débat comme un aigle blessé,
Portant comme le mien, sur son aile asservie,
Tout un monde fatal, écrasant et glacé. (MB. 1-4)

The oppressive nature of contemporary society represses Eva's
natural buoyancy — 'Ta Pensée a des bonds comme ceux des
gazelles' (MB. 246) — which can only function removed from
the prevalent social environment. Such is also the fate of
Samson, betrayed and morally burdened by the false Dalila far
more than any physical weight has ever burdened him:

Mais enfin je suis las. — J'ai l'âme si pesante,
Que mon corps gigantesque et ma tête puissante
Qui soutiennent le poids des colonnes d'airain
Ne la peuvent porter avec tout son chagrin. (CS. 93-96)

The weight carried by Prince Trubetskoi is the very tangible one
of the prisoner's ball and chain (W. 34-35). But again the burden
is not merely physical, but moral — 'la race des Slaves / Doit
porter et le joug et le nom des esclaves' (W. 47-48) — for his
family must bear the spiritual consequences, according to the
Czar's ruling: 'Un esclave a besoin d'un marteau, non d'un
livre' (W. 75). In the barbarism of her natural state the Indian of
'La Sauvage' is weighed down by her child, 'un poids / Qu'elle
baise' (S. 31-32), and she too offers herself to the prisoner to be
'Esclave de tes fils et de tes filles blanches' (S. 129), for she
understands no other way of behaving until she accepts the law

of civilisation, of which the weight is ultimately illusory (S. 161-62).

In this poem, as in others, notably 'La Flûte' and 'La Bouteille à la mer', Vigny also introduces the allied concept of oppression by the elements, in the form of the storm. The desert from which the Indian woman is fleeing echoes to the sound of an oncoming storm — 'L'orage sonne au loin, le bois va se courber' (S. 23). In 'La Flûte', the 'flots ... déserts' (F. 60) are specifically equated with the world of materialism from which the poet and Eva take flight in 'La Maison du berger':

> L'océan du travail si chargé de tempêtes
> Où chaque vague emporte et brise mille têtes. (F. 61-62)

In 'La Bouteille à la mer' the bottle survives the storm which destroys the poet-captain, of whom we are told that 'le vent l'emporte' (BM. 8) and 'le courant l'écrase et le roule dans sa course' (BM. 12). This poem offers the fullest discussion of man's necessary reaction to the weight of the 'destinée' of the old world:

> Il voit les masses d'eau, les toise et les mesure,
> Les méprise en sachant qu'il en est écrasé,
> Soumet son âme au poids de la matière impure.
>
> (BM. 15-17)

The poet-captain's smile as he dies (BM. 99) illustrates his confidence that the bottle will win through as a harbinger of man's new 'destinée', despite the odds. The images of weight give way here, with the engulfing of the ship — 'le brick englouti' (BM. 107) — to images of geographical slavery, as the 'glaçons' (BM. 113) try to hold the bottle back. More fortunate here, however, than the prince and princess in the permanently ice-bound Siberian wastes of 'Wanda', the bottle achieves its liberation, the transformation of the concept of 'destinée' (again we should note that the movement is back from the *geographical* New World to the Old):

Elle attend que l'été, changeant ses destinées,
Vienne ouvrir le rempart des glaces obstinées.

(BM. 117-18)

The weight of the material world is likewise ultimately negated
in 'La Flûte', where it is embodied in the concept of the
inadequate construction of the instrument which impedes the
free and full expression of the soul through harmony. Here it is
the 'bois lourd' (F. 119) of the flute which is at fault, and the
poem, although it implies that only after death can 'la sainte
égalité des esprits du Seigneur' (F. 132) be achieved, demon-
strates nonetheless that an awareness of the nature of the
inadequacy can assist in overcoming it, since we are told of the
flautist that, as he plays the 'Salve Regina'

Son regard attendri paraissait inspiré,
La note était plus juste et le souffle assuré. (F. 139-40)

To the various types of weight imagery is added that of darkness, which again may be perceived in either physical or metaphorical terms. The physical settings of a number of the poems
are symbolically nocturnal: the forests of the New World
condemn their inhabitants to 'd'éternelles nuits' (S. 3),
Samson's final encounter with Dalila's treachery takes place by
night (CS. 3), as does the death of the wolf:

Les nuages couraient sur la lune enflammée
Comme sur l'incendie on voit fuir la fumée,
Et les bois étaient noirs jusques à l'horizon. (ML. 1-3)

In each of these poems we find the attendant image of fire — the
'brûlants soleils' (S. 3) which are the only, albeit occasional,
illumination in the forest of 'La Sauvage', the 'fournaise du
jour' (CS. 4) of 'La Colère de Samson', which we are told the
night cannot mitigate, and the specific association of the two in
the lines from 'La Mort du loup' quoted above. 'Wanda' also
conforms to this pattern, although in a slightly less orthodox
way. The princess tells Wanda: 'Je descendrai vivante au

tombeau du mineur' (W. 49), and we later learn that the four children have grown up in these nocturnal conditions (W. 63). The image of fire is, however, more poignantly embodied in the 'diamants en feu' (W. 10) of her tiara: here Vigny's constant symbol of the new order, the 'diamant', has paradoxically and ironically been transmuted by the addition of the attribute 'en feu' into a representation of the old order. The tiara that marked the princess out as a member of the nobility portends by the nature of its brilliance the obliteration of that class. The references to the 'perles noires' (W. 6) and Wanda's hands which 'par ces rubis', likewise the legacy of the princess, 'semblent ensanglantées' (W. 3) underline the point.

This imagery, however, takes on its fullest significance and ramifications in 'Le Mont des oliviers', of which the opening section is laden with recurrent images of darkness, mourning and death:

> Alors il était nuit et Jésus marchait seul,
> Vêtu de blanc ainsi qu'un mort de son linceul...
> Triste jusqu'à la mort; l'œil sombre et ténébreux...
> — Mais le ciel reste noir, et Dieu ne répond pas...
> Mais un sommeil de mort accable les apôtres...
> Mais un nuage en deuil s'étend comme le voile
> D'une veuve et ses plis entourent le désert...
> — Et la Terre trembla, sentant la pesanteur
> Du Sauveur qui tombait aux pieds du créateur.
> (MO. 1-2, 6, 13, 19, 24-25, 33-34)

Vigny's achievement in this poem is the use of the device of the pathetic fallacy where the depiction of the setting mirrors the saviour's psychological state. The mirror effect which Vigny achieves in 'Le Mont des oliviers' is to extend the concept of Jesus as 'le fils de l'homme' (MO. 21) to produce a series of image parallels between Jesus's own situation and feelings and those of the world for which he intercedes. Thus his own fear and sadness — 'la crainte / Serra son cœur mortel' (MO. 27-28), 'triste jusqu'à la mort' (MO. 6) — are paralleled by those experienced by all humanity at this juncture: 'la Terre a peur'

(MO. 39), 'la Mort... / Attristant la Nature (MO. 111-12); and just as Jesus 'crie avec effroi' (MO. 17), so the sound of 'gémissement' (MO. 78) emerges from humankind. The weight of anguish Jesus feels — 'la pesanteur / Du Sauveur' (MO. 33-34) — is matched by the evil that 'pèse de partout sur la Création' (MO. 90). And the unrelieved darkness of the night sky — 'un nuage en deuil s'étend comme le voile / D'une veuve, et ses plis entourent le désert' (MO. 24-25) — finds its equivalent on Earth in 'ce manteau de misère / Qui l'entoure à grands plis' (MO. 84-85), in its fear 'de rester seule et veuve' (MO. 39), and in the image of 'son sein desséché' (MO. 41), aridity being the characteristic of the 'désert'. Finally, as Jesus 'cherche au firmament / Si l'Ange ne luit pas au fond de quelque étoile' (MO. 22-23), so too humanity seeks to know 'si les Nations sont des femmes guidées / Par les étoiles d'or des divines idées' (MO. 119-20). Not until the end of the poem does Vigny bring the two levels together, when Earth (and by extension humanity) is characterised as 'sans clartés, sans astre et sans aurore, / Et sans clartés de l'âme' (MO. 139-40), prior to the situation being resolved both for Jesus and mankind by the arrival of Judas; once again, the image of fire, 'la torche de Judas' (MO. 142) makes its appearance. Here, as in 'La Colère de Samson', it signals, not security and rescue, but betrayal and destruction. It is, moreover, the 'dents de feu' (MB. 68) of the railway engine's furnace that lead to the accident at Versailles in 'La Maison du berger', and the waters around Tierra del Fuego, 'la Terre-de-Feu' (BM. 37) that destroy the poet-captain and his ship in 'La Bouteille à la mer'.

It is therefore very important to note that images of fire and images of light should not be confused. Whereas fire represents the grip of metaphysical 'destinée' and the old God, light represents the victory of man over the forces that oppress him and the institution of a secular 'destinée'. Its absence, in the form of the 'étoile' (D. 9) is what epitomises the misery of the human condition in 'Les Destinées': in the companion poem, 'Le Mont des oliviers', Jesus, as we have seen, 'cherche au firmament / Si l'Ange ne luit pas au fond de quelque étoile' (MO. 22-23), and the absence of 'l'amour, son étoile fidèle'

(MB. 6) similarly characterises the dismal nature of existence for Eva in 'La Maison du berger'. Elsewhere in the poems, however, the presence of light explicitly or implicitly betokens the dawning of a new age.

This point may be seen at its most literal in 'La Maison du berger', where Vigny uses precisely such an image to indicate the gradual emergence of mankind from barbarism (MB. 208-10). This light in its full splendour is that cast by the 'diamant', piercing through the sterile demagogic squabbling, the 'éternel brouillard' (O. 123) of 'Les Oracles', or that created by the daylight which streams into the pioneer's house in 'La Sauvage', symbolically set apart from the dense foliage of the 'forêt sauvage' (S. 26) of North America: 'Fermée à l'ennemi, la maison s'ouvre au jour' (S. 67). It is the sun that shines on the embarcation of the sailors in 'La Bouteille à la mer' (BM. 61), and which prefigures the eventual homecoming of the bottle itself, a point underlined by the introduction of the key 'diamant' image:

> Un jour, tout était calme, et la mer Pacifique
> Par ses vagues d'azur, d'or et de diamant,
> Renvoyait ses splendeurs au soleil du tropique.
>
> (BM. 120-22)

It is the light that, to the inadequacy of the flautist in 'La Flûte' acts as the equivalent of the illumination of St Paul on the road to Damascus:

> L'idée à l'horizon est à peine entrevue,
> Que sa lumière écrase et fait ployer ma vue. (F. 73-74)

It is, finally, the light proclaimed by Eva in 'L'Age d'or de l'avenir': she, unlike the flautist, is capable of sustaining the impact of its brilliance:

> Le rideau s'est levé devant mes yeux débiles,
> La lumière s'est faite et j'ai vu ses splendeurs.
>
> (AOA, 1-2)

This light — and Vigny's syntax makes it clear that it is a secular version of God's creation of light in Genesis — ultimately counterbalances and destroys the oppressive weight of the meta-physical 'destinée' that kept man in chains:

> Il sait que l'univers l'écrase et le dévore;
> Plus grand que l'univers qu'il juge et qui l'ignore,
> Le Berger a lui-même éclairé sa maison. (AOA, 12-14)

The image of light is, of course, impossible to dissociate from those other more tangible symbols of the future. The 'perle de la pensée' (MB. 134) is possessed of a 'lueur mystérieuse et pâle' (MB. 139), and is destined to 'briller sur un front mâle' (MB. 138), whereas the 'diamant sans rival' (MB. 204) has a similar mission — 'que tes feux illuminent / Les pas lents et tardifs de l'humaine raison' (MB. 204-05). The 'Post-scriptum' to 'Les Oracles' confirms the interpretation of all these images, with its insistence that 'Le cristal, c'est la Vue et la Clarté du JUSTE' (O. 113), and its definition of 'le DIAMANT' as 'le plus brillant trésor et le plus dur' (O. 133). All these images of light have been selected for their attendant qualities of durability and permanence, as we have already noted.

So it can be argued that *Les Destinées* constitutes a collection of poetry of which the apparently disparate nature is ultimately illusory. Such an observation applies equally to 'forme' and to 'fond': the developmental coherence of theme and ideology is matched by persistent recurrence of various sets of images. I should now like to move to a consideration of more specifically formal concerns, and illustrate some of the ways in which Vigny achieves the reflection of sense in sonority in the versification of *Les Destinées*.

8. *Poetic Form in* Les Destinées

Critics have tended to take refuge in Vigny's own apparent sub-ordination of form to content. Indeed M. Gilman goes to the logical extreme of this approach and asks whether indeed prose was not a more natural vehicle for Vigny than verse. Yet this is to betray the poet's own tenaciously held theories. Certainly he subscribed to the concept of a hierarchy in which content was placed much higher than form:

> La forme extérieure n'est rien qu'un vêtement convenable qui se ploie, se courbe ou s'élève au gré de l'idée fonda-mentale; et toute la construction de l'édifice avec l'habileté de ses lignes ne fait que servir de parure à cette idée, con-sacrer sa durée et demeurer son plus parfait symbole. (7, I, p.866)

But he was not prepared to dispense with verse as his chosen medium. 'La poésie n'est que dans les vers et non ailleurs' (7, II, p.1185), he noted in his *Journal*; and again, 'Tous les grands problèmes de l'humanité peuvent être discutés dans la forme des vers' (7, II, p.1204). And, if Vigny has had his detractors as a poetic technician, he has had his supporters, including, most intriguingly, Verlaine, who wrote in 1865: 'Pour le vers qui est toute une atmosphère, tout un monde ... je ne connais à Baudelaire, parmi les modernes, de rival qu'Alfred de Vigny'. Rarely, however, are such eulogies complemented by any attempt to demonstrate *how* Vigny achieves his effects. To make that attempt is a process fraught with difficulties, and which to some degree is bound to lead to accusations of subjectivism on the part of the critic. Ultimately, however, this cannot constitute an acceptable objection to the endeavour.

Of the eleven poems that make up *Les Destinées*, five, grouped together in the middle of the collection, are written in alexandrines not further subdivided into stanzas, five are in alexandrines subdivided into stanzas of seven lines each, and one, the liminal poem, is in alexandrines grouped in 'terza rima'. Since the poems in stanzas are all, without exception, later in date than the others, it is clear that Vigny felt this form particularly congenial to his concept of philosophical poetry. It also characterises the addendum to 'Le Mont de oliviers', the stanza entitled 'Le Silence', and 'L'Age d'or de l'avenir'. There is no experimentation with metre in the manner of the *Poèmes antiques et modernes*: even in the least serious poem, 'La Flûte', with its echoes of self-irony, Vigny never deviates from the alexandrine. Moreover, where the seven-line stanza is used, the rhyme-scheme never varies: it is always *a b a b c c b*. The rejected first seven-line stanza of 'Les Destinées' conforms to this pattern. 'Les Destinées' has a progressive rhyme-scheme of considerable complexity, analysed in some detail by M. Tournier in his edition: he invites us to see it as a 'structure parfaitement symbolique' (*6*, p.37), but offers an analysis of that structure which strikes me as rather tortuous and contrived. Yet it is clear that Vigny did not use the 'terza rima' form by chance: the existence of the rejected seven-line introductory stanza proves this. It seems probable, in view of the fact that this is the poem in which images of weight are at their most prominent, that Vigny was seeking a form to convey this idea, and in consequence rejected the seven-line stanza as too measured and discursive, insufficiently persistent and relentless. This is the view of S. Haig:

'Terza rima' is a self-perpetuating form that is unremitting in its *enchaînement*; it progresses, or rather moves forward, only within the strict limitations of predetermined repetition, and it is no doubt the notion of illusory change — for it cannot break with its own past — that makes it appropriate for this poem. (*19*, p.105)

So here Vigny gives us a plodding, repetitive rhythm to indicate the plodding, repetitive nature of man's condition, underlining the point by the sonorities he uses: heavy vowel sounds, [u] and the nasals, harsh consonants, [k] (sometimes linked with [R]) and [p], internal rhymes and repetitions, possibly including false rhymes such as [e] and [ɛ], or [o] and [õ]. We can see all these devices in operation if we look at the first three stanzas:

De*p*uis le *p*remier *j*our de la *cré*ation,
Les *p*ieds lourds *et p*uissants de *chaque* Destin*ée*
*P*esaient *sur chaque* tête *et sur* toute action.

Chaque front se *c*ourbait *et* traçait sa *j*ournée,
*C*omme le front d'*un* bœuf creuse *un* sill*on* *p*rofond
*S*ans dé*p*asser la *p*ierre *où* sa ligne *est* born*ée*.

*C*es froides dé*i*tés li*ai*ent le *j*oug de *p*lomb
*S*ur le *c*râne *et* les yeux des Hommes leurs esclaves,
*T*ous errants, *sans* ét*oï*le, *en un* désert *sans* fond.
                                                                (D. 1-9)

It is particularly striking that by line 9 the monotony and repetitiousness are almost complete (the line is dominated by nasals) with the exception of the positive keyword 'étoile', whose vowel (and frigidity) are, however, anticipated in 'froides' (D. 7). But in this mournful state of affairs 'étoile' is governed by the preposition 'sans' which negates it and which forms part of the complex of repetitions (first used in line 6, it recurs twice in line 9), which irresistibly conveys the overriding impression of hopelessness.

It is thus fair to say that in the poem Vigny's use of a specific stanza form contributes to some extent to convey his meaning. The most pessimistic poem of the collection, it is also the only one to be written in a form which effectively reinforces that pessimism. It can also be argued that the retention of this 'terza rima' to narrate the coming of Christ, where the term 'le jeune athlète' (D. 24) might well lead us to expect the introduction of a more joyous metre, is a further illustration on a formal level of the thematic message of the poem, that Christ's coming in fact changes nothing. Significantly, all we get is a sort of galvanic hiccough — 'Secoua sa poussière' (D. 23) — before the measured tread of the lines resumes. Apart from 'Les

Destinées', however, it seems clear that Vigny's persistent attachment, first to the sequential form of the alexandrine and thereafter to the seven-line stanza, underlines the point that his main concern is to convey *meaning*, specifically in terms of his own views on philosophical problems.

Even so, there is little doubt that Vigny's poetic art is sufficiently in evidence to negate Sainte-Beuve's original judgment that the collection represents a 'déclin bien soutenu'. This is not to suggest that Vigny still cannot, on occasion, write badly: rather that by restricting his range he reduces the number of pitfalls that lie in wait for him. We still come across the relatively frequent use of inversion, horribly cluttered lines such as 'Le Passant au Passant montre au ciel tout point noir' (O. 9), and the more occasional use of tortured syntax such as 'Il porte du Génie et transmet les empreintes' (O. 131) — all of which can make this poetry sound very laboured. Now and again indeed, we find passages of profound obscurity bordering on complete incoherence, such as the quite disastrous sixth stanza of 'Les Oracles'. On the other hand, I am much less inclined to concur with certain received critical opinion that the 'digression' on the railway train, which occupies the centre of the first section of 'La Maison du berger' is an aesthetic blemish, and that the poem is 'spoiled' by its inclusion. True, it clashes with the supremely harmonious evocation of the beauties of nature, one of the pinnacles of Vigny's poetic achievement:

> La Nature t'attend dans un silence austère;
> L'herbe élève à tes pieds son nuage des soirs,
> Et le soupir d'adieu du soleil à la terre
> Balance les beaux lys comme des encensoirs.
> La forêt a voilé ses colonnes profondes,
> La montagne se cache, et sur les pâles ondes
> Le saule a suspendu ses chastes reposoirs. (MB. 29-35)

The effect of this magical stanza is achieved mainly by the constant repetition of the sibilants, which produces an impression of tranquil mystery. Added to this is the muted echo effect of nasal vowels, especially in line 29 (att*en*d / *un* sil*en*ce) and lines 32-35 (bal*a*nce / *e*ncensoirs; prof*o*ndes / m*o*ntagnes / *o*ndes; susp*e*ndu), which contributes to the impression that, in Baudelaire's words, 'La Nature est un temple où de vivants piliers / Laissent parfois sortir de confuses paroles': the echo effect is that of the church which the lexis describes (encensoirs, colonnes, reposoirs).

This, then, is to be the temple of Vigny's God, a far cry from the God he has rejected, the 'Dieu de l'or' (MB. 84) served by the railway train. Self-evidently, the evocation of the realm of the God of materialism must clash as harshly as possible with the evocation of the realm of the new God, must be as cacophonous as the other was euphonious. The section devoted to the railway train is therefore neither disfiguring, nor a digression: it fulfils a vital function in the poem. Vigny also contrives to suggest, in the terms 'vapeur foudroyante' (MB. 64) and the reference to 'le taureau de fer qui fume, souffle et beugle' (MB. 78), the sound of the engine (by use of [v] and [f]), to add to the cacophonous effect of the collocation of the words employed.

Yet, before we consider this, we should note a second major contrast in this poem. Nature is contrasted not only with materialistic society, but with itself devoid of the presence of Eva. Now the evocation of the industrial city contrasts violently with the almost incantatory effect of the description of nature inhabited by Eva. Tranquillity gives places to hustle and bustle:

> Que Dieu guide à son but la vapeur foudroyante
> Sur le fer des chemins qui traversent les monts,
> Qu'un Ange soit debout sur sa forge bruyante,
> Quand elle va sous terre ou fait trembler les ponts
> Et, de ses dents de feu, dévorant ses chaudières,
> Transperce les cités et saute les rivières,
> Plus vite que le cerf dans l'ardeur de ses bonds!
>
> (MB. 64-70)

Here the effect is of haste: harsh sounds tumbling one on top of the other, the almost total absence of internal rhymes, and a predominance (in lines 68 and 70) of [d] sounds reminiscent of a train rattling along the rails. Nature without Eva is different again, possessed of a marmoreal hardness, a frigid impersonality:

Elle me dit: 'Je suis l'impassible théâtre
Que ne peut remuer le pied de ses acteurs;
Mes marches d'émeraude et mes parvis d'albâtre,
Mes colonnes de marbre ont les dieux pour sculpteurs.
Je n'entends ni vos cris ni vos soupirs; à peine
Je sens passer sur moi la comédie humaine
Qui cherche en vain au ciel ses muets spectateurs.

(MB. 281-87)

Here all is clinical: almost no muting nasals, a predominance of measured, hard dentals and labial plosives ([d], [t], [b], [p]), the menacing roll of [R], the scornful disdain of [m]. The hardness of the sounds reflects that of the substances evoked — emerald, alabaster, marble — and the consequently required activity of sculpting to make any impression. Here, then, we have linguistic devices used to complement the meaning of the poem, the harshness and inexorability of the old God conveyed in the sonorities of Vigny's poetic language.

Yet in a sense, any attempt to define Vigny's poetic genius must pinpoint the reasons why so many critics have abstained. It is an attempt to define the indefinable. Perhaps E. Estève comes close to the truth when he writes of 'un certain nombre de beaux vers isolés, de grands vers profonds' (*14*, p.273). With some of these 'beaux vers' it is possible to grasp at the impression they produce: they enshrine with a deceptive simplicity a truth that we have ourselves experienced or of which we perceive the intrinsic beauty and would ideally wish to imitate. It is as if Vigny has suddenly, quite unexpectedly, been able to put into words a reality, a truth for which we have ineffectually been seeking. In this respect, each one of these lines constitutes that 'Trésor de la pensée et de l'expérience' (BM. 150), which for Vigny was the reality of poetry. Each reader will have his or her own 'favourite' lines for this reason. But I know of no poet other than Vigny who can produce such profound effects with such economy of means, as in the following lines:

Tout homme a vu le mur qui borne son esprit. (F. 108)

J'aime la majesté des souffrances humaines. (MB. 321)

Seul le silence est grand; tout le reste est faiblesse.
                                                    (ML. 78)

Gémir, pleurer, prier est également lâche. (ML. 85)

Sur la pierre des morts croît l'arbre de grandeur.
                                                    (BM. 168)

Aimez ce que jamais on ne verra deux fois. (MB. 308)

Vous qui savez aimer, vous feriez comme moi. (W. 28)

Sacrifice, ô toi seul peut-être es la vertu! (W. 98)

I could go on. In some of these lines, I think it is undeniable that there is a vibrancy of personal commitment that communicates itself from the poet to the reader, and with a discretion that makes a poet like Musset appear shallow in comparison. It is worth remembering that the poet who could write the hopelessly convoluted and pompous stanzas of 'Les Oracles' could also convey a wealth of emotion and experience in the lines where a sailor close to death remembers the woman he left behind:

Un autre y voit Marseille. Une femme se lève,
Court au port et lui tend un mouchoir de la grève,
Et ne sent pas ses pieds enfoncés dans la mer.
                                                    (BM. 75-77)

In the words of Verlaine, 'Tout le reste est littérature'.

Conclusion

In the world of the late twentieth century, the Romantics can sometimes cut a rather sorry figure. The grandiose schemes and utopian visions of Lamartine, Hugo, George Sand and their numerous, if less celebrated, contemporaries may appear to us as embodiments of a vaporous and irrational optimism, as hopelessly at odds with the realities of our time as, we see in retrospect, they were at odds with the trends of their own. On the other hand, we can find little sympathy for the somewhat spineless self-pity of Musset, and may view Gautier's retreat towards Parnassianism as a derogation from the moral responsibilities of art in society. In this perspective, Vigny, if not entirely 'modern', nonetheless communicates an intellectual toughness, a grim perception of what life is like, that render him more acceptable to our disillusioned generation than his contemporaries. Like Corneille, a writer he much admired, he does not try to buck the problems he encounters, but confronts them and seeks an honourable solution.

This is not to say that his work does not contain much that is dated and unacceptable. His views on colonialism would not find many adherents in our century, though they were widely held in his own. His paternalism is out of vogue. The kindest comment we can pass on his attitudes to woman is that they are all too redolent of a bygone age: even when they apparently put her on a pedestal, as in 'La Maison du berger', 'La Sauvage' and 'Wanda', they cannot conceal the necessity, in Vigny's eyes, of her subservience to man. It is significant that her role in 'L'Esprit pur', Vigny's poetic and personal testament, is passive, almost non-existent: she is present only to applaud the poet's self-celebration. Amateur psychoanalysts will not have failed to note, on the other hand, that the cruel and repressive 'destinées' are women, and that 'La Colère de Samson' is a vicious, not to say hysterical, outburst against a woman whom he considered to have failed him. We must be grateful for his posthumous reputation that he had the good taste (and good sense) not to publish it in his lifetime, although his inclusion of it in the final plan of 27 May 1863 leads us to wonder whether only death prevented him from making it public.

Set against these considerations, and ultimately transcending them, we find in *Les Destinées* values which have stood the test of the years. We find a deeply moving (because deeply felt) indictment of a pernicious world order. Today, no less than in Vigny's day, we read of situations where unjust and oppressive regimes deny individual liberties, just as they do in 'Wanda', or situations where senseless aggression destroys opportunities for individual and collective happiness, as in 'La Sauvage' and 'La Bouteille à la mer'. And how depressingly familiar to us are Vigny's excoriations of the self-interest and corruption of politicians in 'La Maison du berger' and 'Les Oracles'.

Yet this is the dark side of the coin. Vigny does not offer us a diet of bleak and unrelieved pessimism, and to set against his indictment of the existing world order, we have a deeply moving (because deeply felt) affirmation of the values of the human heart and spirit. Once the accretions of nineteenth-century didacticism are stripped away, Vigny's values are ours, or what ours ought to be. Like Voltaire, he has no real illusions about his fellow-men, but his ultimate belief that man need not always be a wolf to man, and that progress is possible, less through technology than through morality, that man is, in the words of George Sand, 'perfectible dans le bien, corrigible dans le mal', constitutes his most enduring message to posterity. As we might infer from the last stanza of 'L'Esprit pur', it is the epitaph he would have wanted.

Bibliography

An enormous amount has been written, and is still being written, about Vigny, and it is impossible to include more than a small portion of it in a selective bibliography of this nature. I therefore make no apology for listing only books, sections of books and articles dealing exclusively with Vigny, and which I have found to be of material assistance, even though this necessitates some ruthless exclusions. Brief comments on the primary sources and editions will be found in the Note at the beginning of this volume.

A. PRIMARY SOURCES AND EDITIONS

1. A. de Vigny, *Poèmes antiques et modernes* and *Les Destinées*, edited by A. Jarry (Paris, Gallimard, Collection 'Poésie', 1973).
2. ——, *Œuvres poétiques*, edited by J.-P. Saint-Gérand (Paris, Garnier-Flammarion, 1978).
3. ——, *Les Destinées*, edited by V.-L. Saulnier (Geneva, Droz, 1946).
4. ——, *Les Destinées*, edited by P.-G. Castex (Paris, S.E.D.E.S., 1968).
5. ——, *Les Destinées*, edited by A. Bouvet (Paris, Bordas, 1971).
6. ——, *Les Destinées*, edited by M. Tournier (Paris, Larousse, 1972).
7. ——, *Œuvres complètes*, edited by F. Baldensperger (Paris, Gallimard, Bibl. de la Pléiade, 1948-50, 2 vols).
8. ——, *Mémoires inédits*, edited by J. Sangnier (Paris, Gallimard, 1958).

B. SECONDARY SOURCES

9. P. Bénichou, 'Vigny et l'architecture des *Destinées*', *RHLF*, 80 (1980), 41-64. A meticulous and methodical article, chronicling the gradual evolution of the collection, and arguing that the ultimate ordering of the poems, although established by Vigny, makes no logical sense.
10. G. Bonnefoy, *La Pensée religieuse et morale d'Alfred de Vigny* (Geneva, Slatkine, 1971). Reprint of the original Paris edition of 1944. Exhaustively (and exhaustingly) documented doctoral thesis, a work of rather ponderous and indigestible erudition. Not quite complete at the author's death, consequently less full on *Les Destinées* than on earlier works.
11. P.-G. Castex, *Alfred de Vigny* (Paris, Hatier, Coll. Connaissance des Lettres, 1957). Excellent, highly recommendable short study of 'l'homme et l'œuvre', the ideal beginner's guide to Vigny.
12. ——, 'Le Mythe d'Eva dans *Les Destinées*. Etude de genèse', *L'Information littéraire*, 32 (1980), 12-21 and 58-67. Very informative

double article, dealing not only with the identity of Eva, but also with the elaboration of 'La Maison du berger' and Vigny's early projects for the collection which became *Les Destinées*. Usefully read in conjunction with *18*.

13. —— (ed.), *Relire 'Les Destinées' d'Alfred de Vigny* (Paris, S.E.D.E.S., 1980). A curate's egg of a collection. There are some well-argued pieces (notably those by M. Cambien, C. Crossley and P. Viallaneix), but it is difficult to avoid the impression that in some other cases the all-too-familiar linguistic smokescreen conceals an example of the Emperor's new clothes.

14. E. Estève, *Alfred de Vigny: sa pensée et son art* (Paris, Garnier, 1923). A sound, if now rather dated survey, and notable for its attempt to implement the promise of its title, despite the fact that the observations on 'art' are of a rather generalised nature.

15. P. Flottes, *La Pensée politique et sociale d'Alfred de Vigny* (Paris, Les Belles-Lettres, 1927). Primarily an intellectual biography. I wonder if it does not tend to see Vigny's poetry too much in terms of contemporary political considerations: some of the interpretations seem a little erratic.

16. ——, *Vigny et sa fortune littéraire* (St-Médard en Jalles, Ducros, 1970). Useful survey of the evolution of Vigny's reputation over the years since his first writings were published to the present day.

17. F. Germain, *L'Imagination d'Alfred de Vigny* (Paris, Corti, 1961). The most sustained work of erudition ever to have appeared on Vigny. A quite remarkable survey of Vigny's imaginative processes, culminating in a vivid picture of a confused and rather unhappy man. The author's knowledge of Vigny's work is comprehensive and masterly.

18. H. Guillemin, *M. de Vigny, homme d'ordre et poète* (Paris, Gallimard, 1955). A valuable and entertaining set of studies on various aspects of Vigny's life and work. The chapter entitled 'La Genèse des *Destinées*', although in some degree superseded by more recent research, is still useful.

19. S. Haig, 'The double register of 'Les Destinées'', *Studi francesi*, 22 (1978), 104-06. Brief but lucid article on the versification of this problematical poem.

20. A. Jarry, 'Vigny 1979', *Romantisme*, 25-26 (1979), 217-41. A most useful article, giving a *résumé* of the state of Vigny studies up till 1979, and helpfully listing the results of the most recent research.

21. E. Lauvrière, *Alfred de Vigny, sa vie et son œuvre* (Paris, Grasset, 1945, 2 vols). Heavily documented, but rather ill-organised book, without a great deal of relevance to say about the poetry, but quite useful as a collection of contemporary 'témoignages' on Vigny.

22. P. Moreau, *Les 'Destinées' d'Alfred de Vigny* (Paris, SFELT, 1936). An excellent short study on the genesis, thought and art of *Les Destinées*, benefiting from an attempt to evaluate the poems as poetry as well as to offer a summary of the ideas they embody.

23. J.-P. Richard, *Etudes sur le romantisme* (Paris, Seuil, 1970), pp.161-76. A fascinating article on the formal aspects of 'La Maison du berger', illustrating the way in which such an approach can lead to a conclusion similar to that involving a study of Vigny's 'ideas'. Rather pretentiously written, though.

24. J. Sungolowsky, *Alfred de Vigny et le dix-huitième siècle* (Paris, Nizet, 1968). This contrives to be a useful conspectus of the central themes of Vigny's *œuvre*, linking them back to the seminal figures of eighteenth-century thought. A modest and unpretentious work.

25. M. Toesca, *Vigny, ou la passion de l'honneur* (Paris, Hachette, 1972). Full, quite entertaining but over-long 'biographie romancée', con-centrating on the events of the poet's life, but relating them in some degree to his writings. Not always very accurate.

26. P. Viallaneix, *Vigny par lui-même* (Paris, Seuil, 1970). This is another excellent introductory volume, which eschews the strictly chronological approach adopted by P.-G. Castex (*11*) in favour of a thematic approach. It covers all aspects of Vigny's output, although it tends to give more attention to the prose works.

CRITICAL GUIDES TO FRENCH TEXTS

edited by
Roger Little, Wolfgang van Emden, David Williams